"The "beauty of virtue" is not something most Protestants think about. But it is the theme of this beautiful treatise written by the seventeenth-century Anglican poet and theologian Thomas Traherne, whose writings are now being discovered as gold suddenly appearing at the bottom of a long-lost cave. Colin Chan Redemer is a masterful writer and translator whose new rendition of Traherne's Christian Ethics is a must-read for Anglicans and all Christians who want to "leave elementary doctrine" and go on to "maturity" that relishes the beauty of holiness."

—Gerald McDermott, *Retired Anglican Chair of Divinity at Beeson Divinity School*

THE SHINING
HUMAN CREATURE

CHRISTIAN ETHICS VOL. 1

CHRISTIAN ETHICS

OR
DIVINE MORALITY:
OPENING THE WAY
TO BLESSEDNESS BY THE RULES
OF VIRTUE AND REASON

by Thomas Traherne

Edited by Colin Chan Redemer

For Felicity

ISBN: 1-949716-16-3

ISBN-13: 978-1-949716-16-0

Front cover image is "The Well-stocked Kitchen, with Jesus in the House of Martha and Mary in the Background" by Joachim Bueckelaer, 1566

Cover design by Rachel Rosales, Orange Peal Design

Proofread and typeset by Mikael Good

TABLE OF CONTENTS

INTRODUCTION

Colin Chan Redemer

Introduction to the Man

DESPITE being praised by the likes of Thomas Merton and Dorothy Sayers, and possessing a prose style C. S. Lewis called "almost the most beautiful…in English," the poet, pastor, and theologian Thomas Traherne (1636/37–1674) was virtually unknown in his own lifetime.[1]

The story of how this came to be requires some telling. It marks him out from other luminaries who are published in the Library of Early English Protestantism; figures like Richard Hooker and John Davenant loomed large in their day. Their works formed the backbone of the curriculum taught to the great and the good for over a century after their deaths, and if they are forgotten now, that is only among the general populace; learned men still know of their lives and works.

Traherne's story is different. He composed a mere two volumes for publication in his lifetime.[2] The first, *Roman*

---

[1] C. S. Lewis to Arthur Greeves, Dec 23, 1941, *The Collected Letters of C. S. Lewis*, 3 vols. (London: HarperOne, 2004), 2:504.

[2] I should add "that we know of." I shall cover both unpublished works by Traherne and published works of which Traherne may be the author below.

Forgeries (1673), is a polemical tract covering the various documents regarding the first 420 years of the Church's history, opposing the papal claims and exposing the ways in which various forged documents were used to support the papacy throughout history.[3] The second book is that which you hold in your hand, *Christian Ethicks: or divine Morality, opening the Way to Blessedness, by the Rules of Virtue and Reason* (1675). This text was written at the request of his patron Sir Orlando Bridgeman (1606–74), a great statesman of whom there will be more to say shortly. Bridgeman never had a chance to read the finished text as he died before the writing was complete, in June of 1674, and *Ethicks* was finished and sent to the publishers early in that fall. Traherne at that time was ailing, and died shortly thereafter with the text still yet unpublished. It was published the following year in 1675. A book with no living patron and no living author, whose transmission depended upon the small readership of *Roman Forgeries*, was not likely to be widely read, and so it was not. Few read Traherne in his day and fewer remembered him after. History seemed to have closed on this man who died young and in obscurity.[4]

And there the story might have ended. Traherne fell into the Great River, Time, and vanished. His papers, which he had deeded to his brother Philip, sank in with him. They passed out of knowledge and legend for two hundred years; and even the parts of Traherne's history recounted here

---

[3] It should be noted that, while this is a virulent anti–Roman Catholic text, its existence began out of a conversation between Traherne and a Roman Catholic in the Bodleian Library, as he says in the introduction to the work. It is this author's hope that sharp disputation does not exclude friendship.

[4] I will say more about the contents of this second book below.

were known only to a few, and even they could discover no more. But thankfully, I can carry on the story.

Long after, indeed not very long ago, there lived a man named William T. Brooke (1848–1917), who, on what was likely a winter day in 1897,[5] while perusing the papers of the bookbarrow at Farringdon Road in London, came across some manuscripts which, if not purchased, were shortly to be destroyed.[6] Upon leafing through them he was stunned. These, he thought, must be some lost work of a brilliant man, perhaps the Welsh metaphysical poet Henry Vaughan (1621–95).[7] Brooke bought the manuscript which he then

---

[5] It is likely known only to God precisely when this took place. Secondary sources offer dates that range from 1895 (see *Poetical Works of Thomas Traherne*, ed. Gladys Wade (London: P.J. & A.E. Dobell, 1932)), to specifically April 1897 (see the website of the Catalogue of English Literary Manuscripts 1450–1700, accessed Jan 12 2023, https://celm-ms.org.uk/introductions/TraherneThomas.html#), to the more epistemologically modest claim of 1896–1897 (see, for example, Denise Inge's *Wanting Like A God: Desire and Freedom in the Works of Thomas Traherne* (London: SCM Press, 2009) and also The Oxford Traherne website, accessed Feb 24, 2022, https://oxfordtraherne.org/trahernes-manuscripts/).

[6] For a likely more accurate manuscript transmission history see the Catalogue of English Literary Manuscripts 1450–1700, https://celm-ms.org.uk/introductions/TraherneThomas.html. Some of the claims (e.g., that both manuscripts were found in one day and one place) are disputed.

[7] The speculation that it was a work by Vaughan was high praise indeed. Vaughan, a Welshman, was a physician poet, a tradition stretching from Ctesias and St. Luke to innumerable contemporaries. Like Traherne he, too, would find far greater fame after his death than in his life, but unlike Traherne he had some works which were widely praised in his lifetime. Notable among these is his *Silex Scintillans*, or "the sparking flint," in which, after a near death experience, Vaughan turns his poetic vocation

sold to his friend Dr. Alexander Grosart (1827–99), whom he convinced of his idea of their being of Vaughan's authorship.[8] Together they intended to publish it. However, yet another untimely end interposed; Dr. Grosart died before he and Brooke could bring the text to print. This proved fortuitous.

Before Dr. Grosart's death, Brooke had spoken of his extraordinary find to another bookseller, Bertram Dobell (1842–1914). Dobell bought the late Dr. Grosart's library and studied with great care the manuscript that Brooke had re-discovered. The result of this closer study was Dobell's conviction that Vaughan could not have produced this text. Dobell brought this theory back to Brooke, which triggered in Brooke a memory that he had once edited a volume titled *A Serious and Pathetical Contemplation of the Mercies of God*, and that this volume had contained a poem similar to some of the poetry found in this mystery manuscript. Returning to that source, they uncovered the name "Lord Keeper Bridgeman" as the patron of the author in a preface to the reader explaining who its anonymous author was. Upon further investigation they came to realize that this eminent

---

to the subject of God and the human longing for God and life with him. Vaughan is generally considered to be a member of the "Metaphysical Poets," a name given not entirely in praise by Samuel Johnson to John Donne and a few others. More recent scholars classify not only Vaughan as a member of this group, but Traherne as well. So in the end the speculation was not far from the mark and the Metaphysical Poets are recommended to you for deeper study of the mental world of our author.

[8] The farcical nature of the story grows in that Dr. Grosart, we now know, owned the manuscript he bought off of Brooke back in 1870. How he lost it (and whether, upon purchasing it for a second time in 1896, he recognized it) we do not know. See celm-ms.org.uk/repositories/bodleian-eng-poet-a.html.

man was known to have funded one Thomas Traherne's *Christian Ethicks*.[9] Upon looking inside *Christian Ethicks*, Brooke and Dobell found a portion of the same poem in both the mystery manuscript and in *A Serious and Pathetical Contemplation of the Mercies of God* and in *Christian Ethicks*. The key fit the lock, and the puzzle was solved.[10]

The manuscripts were the work of Thomas Traherne, and we know them as the devotional prose poem *Centuries of Meditation*, as well as other previously unpublished and unknown poetry. Both *Centuries of Meditation* and his poetry began to see light of day in 1903. Since then, these two nearly-lost pieces of his writing have become undisputedly his most famous works, and their publication (and the Indiana-Jones-esque nature of their rediscovery) has led to a whole cottage industry of Traherne republications and scholarship. This has, however, tended to focus attention away from the only two texts which were intended for publication during Traherne's lifetime: *Roman Forgeries* and *Christian Ethicks*. More could be said about the various other texts now believed or argued to have been Traherne's, or of those manuscripts which are of more recent discovery. In the former category we can include anonymously published

---

[9] As I have said, Traherne was virtually unknown and so it is not clear how they came to find out that Bridgeman was Traherne's patron. I assume, though, that by researching Bridgeman, who was a public figure, some record which I cannot uncover surfaced referencing Traherne, possibly the dedication of *Roman Forgeries* to Bridgeman.

[10] For fuller treatment and for the reference on the manuscript transmission story see Gladys Wade, *Thomas Traherne* (New York: Octagon Books, 1969), 3–11. Wade takes creative liberties in the telling and was working with 1940s source materials. See my previous footnotes for more information.

seventeenth-century documents such as the *Hexameron*; in the latter, documents which keep turning up and may be Traherne's—this has happened as recently as 1997 when the Folger Library in Washington, D.C., published a manuscript they attributed to Traherne entitled *The Ceremonial Law*.[11] The disputes over the authorship of many texts is complicated by the fact that Traherne had mastered multiple styles of handwriting, and so there is no one hand which is decisively his.[12] Intriguingly, he is one of only two poets of the seventeenth century whose poetry we have extant in their own hand, the other being John Milton (1608–74). The story will continue, no doubt, but it is the purpose of this volume to bring us back to the source. The good news about the twentieth-century revival of Thomas Traherne is that we can now discern more of the man himself as a result of over a hundred years of scholarship.

As we have noted, it is to Traherne's obscurity in his own time that we owe the great fogginess that still hangs over him. When interest in him was renewed, at first there was confusion about almost all of the facts of his life. Where was he born? When? To what family? How was he educated and how did he make his living? These and other questions have vexed scholars who encounter him and want to know more, but as time passes and more documents turn up, the story has come somewhat into focus. We can say almost for a certainty that he was born in Herefordshire, likely in the year 1637. It was the reign of King Charles I (r. 1625–49),

---

[11] A printed edition of the Folger manuscript of this work can be found in Thomas Traherne, *The Works of Thomas Traherne*, 7 vols. (Rochester: Boydell & Brewer, 2014), vol. 6, 195-242.

[12] Thomas Sluberski, *A Mind in Frame* (Cleveland: Lincoln Library Press, 2008), 52.

and those who know this period of English history know that young Thomas was born into turbulent times.[13] His formative years were lived first in the midst of the English Civil War (1642–51), then under Oliver Cromwell's regime as Lord Protector of the Commonwealth of England, Scotland, and Ireland (1653–58). As a young man in the midst of such turmoil, he went up to Brasenose College, Oxford, probably about age fifteen. He studied there and finished his baccalaureate degree in 1656 before receiving a Master of Arts in 1661, and then a Bachelor of Divinity degree in 1669. Modern Americans are unfamiliar with the Oxford system whereby the B.A. "matriculates" into an M.A. a few years after graduation, sometimes requiring a seated test. Why he went back for the B.D. after the M.A. was awarded is unclear since it seems he was already a practicing minister. Suffice it to say he was dedicated to learning.[14] Of Oxford he says he was educated "at universities in Beautiful Streets and Famous Colleges."[15] Between these degrees, in the time of the Protectorate, he received a nonepiscopal ordination at Credenhill, likely near his hometown in Herefordshire, where he served a congregation. There is sufficient confusion around this that it warrants a moment of consideration: was Traherne a Puritan? Or was he secretly carrying on the practices of the

---

[13] In 1637 Archbishop Laud, Archbishop of Canterbury appointed by Charles I, tried to impose the *Book of Common Prayer* on the Scots, considered by many to be a precursor to the Civil War.

[14] The records of Traherne's education in *Athenae Oxonienses* are less than ideal. Scholars disagree on whether he had to sit for an exam for his M.A. or not. He indisputably continued his studies long after the expectations of his profession and class required.

[15] Sluberski, *Mind in Frame*, 28.

established church? The truth is we do not know and doubtless never will, but it is clear in any case that he was not cut from the cloth of martyrs.[16] After the Restoration in 1660 he received an episcopal ordination, and once more at Credenhill, to serve now as a decidedly episcopalian minister. We don't know how often he was actually present at Credenhill versus Oxford, given the level of pastoral work he was involved in on the one hand and the level of study he was involved in at Oxford on the other. Further, his double-ordination is likely to raise questions among some readers as to his theopolitical opportunism. It is my thesis that such a switch is a sign of at least two things beyond a mere changing of tack with the winds of history. First, the doctrinal distance between Puritans and the established

---

[16] Sluberski, *Mind in Frame*, 16–17. Sluberski describes Traherne's nonepiscopal ordination as "his Puritan presentation to the living at Credenhill," which required recommendations. Those he received were from seven clergymen, "some of whom were leading Puritans in Herefordshire." And in a footnote Sluberski implies this may indicate Traherne's ambivalence towards the established church. Denise Inge claims there were only six clergy who recommended Traherne but notes that five of them were so staunchly Puritan that they were rejected from their livings after the 1660 restoration. Traherne was Puritan enough not to raise their suspicions. This text also contrasts Traherne with his friend Susanna Hopton, whose anti-Puritan sentiment led her to convert to the Roman church for the years of the Protectorate. Denise Inge, *Thomas Traherne: Poetry and Prose* (London: SPCK, 2002), xiv–xxv. Gladys Wade adds that Traherne's education at Oxford was in Brasenose "one of the most thoroughly Puritan" colleges overseen by the just and tolerant Puritan Dr. Greenwood. Wade speculates further that Traherne "probably took the oaths and performed the religious exercises exacted of him by Puritan authority without the slightest feeling that any principles were at stake." Gladys Wade, *Thomas Traherne* (New York: Octagon Books, 1969), 49–50.

Church of England of that era was less significant than it is now commonly assumed to be. In fact the distinction is the stuff of hairsplitting to the point of verging on nonsense, as there were plenty of "Puritan" Episcopalians, and one of the questions around Traherne involves precisely whether this category describes him. Second, Traherne reads as the kind of man who has too many other interests in mind, such as the care of souls and the transmission of the truth, to be bothered overmuch with the nattering of bishops and potentates. As he put it, he was called "to teach immortal Souls the way to Heaven, to sanctify his Sabbaths, to instruct them in the love of a glorious Saviour."[17] It seems clear that in his mind, the path to such work was available to Puritans as well as to those within the episcopalian order. In 1669 he became the chaplain to Sir Orlando Bridgeman, who at that time was Lord Keeper of the Privy Seal, and thus Traherne likely moved at that point to London with him. Traherne served his patron while also serving as the minister of St Mary's Church in Teddington. He died on October 10, 1674 in the home of his patron, with few enough possessions that he could dictate his will on his deathbed.[18] He was buried without fanfare and without a gravestone under the reading desk of St Mary's where he had been serving.[19] He was likely just thirty-eight years old.

---

[17] Sluberski, *Mind in Frame*, 28.

[18] Joseph Foster, "Traherne, Thomas," *Alumni Oxonienses 1500–1714: The Members of the University of Oxford, Their Parentage, Birthplace, and Year of Birth, with a Record of Their Degrees* (Oxford and London: Parker & Co., 1892), accessed online here: https://www.british-history.ac.uk/alumni-oxon/1500-1714/pp1501-1528.

[19] Fuller treatment of his death can be found in the Oxford Dictionary of National Biography, accessed Feb 24 2022,

He was read and commented on only sparsely by the next generation of scholars of divinity. By the eighteenth century, he was ignored. His death, merely a month and a half before his better known peer, John Milton, was unnoticed.

Introduction to Chapters I–VIII

Due to the popularity of the *Centuries*, Traherne is thought of as a Christian Platonist mystic by most of his readers. But most of his readers have not read his *Christian Ethicks*.

This work owes a great deal to the ancient tradition now called "virtue ethics." Indeed, his first three chapters map quite well onto the first two books of Aristotle's *Nicomachean Ethics*. The first covers teleology, or final causality, as applied to man; the second explores the extent and general form of that final cause; the third deals with the definition of virtue and an exploration of some examples of it. Traherne's work is set out not in continuous prose, but in somewhat axiomatic paragraphs, usually of just a few lines (though in some places much longer). They are not isolated aphorisms, however, but build continually upon one another.

I have "virtue ethics" in scare quotes above not because I think it an inapt name, but because those who trade in the term tend to be working in philosophy as a discipline and deploy "virtue ethics" as a counter to something they have named "consequentialism" or "deontology." Whatever any of that means for modern

---

https://www.oxforddnb.com/display/10.1093/ref:odnb/9780198614128.001.0001/odnb-9780198614128-e-38074?rskey=2wKNWV&result=1. This web source draws from Bodl. Oxf., MS Wood F 45, fol. 40.

professional academicians, it would mean almost nothing to Traherne. Traherne, like Aristotle before him, saw ethics not as an academic discipline but as an investigation into how to *live*. Thus, while we see him investigating closely in this text, we also find him practically gushing with gladness at the manifold goodness through which we get to move as we live our lives—not a common feature of academic philosophers. So much the worse for them.

In Chapters IV and V, Traherne departs from walking directly in Aristotle's path and moves into a discourse on the nature of the self.[20] In doing this he is taking the first step in showing us what a transcendent reimagining of virtue ethics must be like. As beings, we are peculiar and require some account. Why isn't virtue natural to us from the day of our birth? Platonic anthropology, made famous by C. S. Lewis as involving a belly, chest, and head, is largely preserved in his account.[21] But what Christianity adds to this is love. Traherne believes all of what we are and all of what we have made of ourselves exists inescapably for the sake of love. What are you without love? he asks, and the question, we discern, is philosophically profound, but also rhetorical. Without love we are nothing. This is the love that spun the sun and stars into being and moves them, yet loves you and wants to dwell in you, and through you desires to

---

[20] Whether the middle books of Aristotle's *Nicomachean Ethics* exploring the virtues as related to various powers of the soul culminating in the comprehensive virtue of justice counts as a psychology is beyond the scope of our present consideration.

[21] "Belly" being ἐπιθυμία or the desiring power; "chest" being θυμός or the competitive power; "head" being λόγος or the rational power. For Lewis's discussion on this, see *The Abolition of Man* (Glasgow: Fount Paperbacks, 1978), 7-20.

fill out creation to the limits of reality with love itself—and God wants us to *know* this about reality.

Chapter VI then moves us into a conversation about the nature of love itself. What is love? We are used to asking this question with flowers, a bottle of wine, and perhaps some candles. But the love Traherne wants to introduce us to is to earthly romance as sun to spark. True love is hotter than we can imagine. But though this highest, divine love is transcendentally incandescent, Traherne tells us it is also supremely gentle, subtle, and kind. And all real Love comes to us from outside ourselves—indeed from outside all of created reality.

From here, we see that Traherne is perhaps not so much following in the footsteps of Aristotle but in those of Thomas Aquinas. Gladys Wade writes with conviction on this point. In an essay from 1931, she lines up samples of writing from Traherne's *Ethics* side-by-side with Aquinas's work to show that he is systematically thinking through problems as his (possible) namesake did.[22] In her words, "he could with the ease of perfect familiarity combine and condense and rearrange into his own pattern the stones from St. Thomas's vast quarry; and this in itself casts an illuminating ray on the intellectual capacity of Traherne, who has sometimes been patronized by his critics as one naively simple and rustically unlearned."[23] Not only was he learned but he was a scholastic in his own right. However, he knew well that, in spite of being cited by Preston and Baxter, the name of Aquinas carried little water in the England of his day. Wade is not the only one to point out

---

[22] Gladys Wade, "St. Thomas Aquinas and Thomas Traherne," *New Blackfriars* 12, no. 140 (November 1931): 668–72.

[23] Wade, "Aquinas and Traherne," 667.

that Traherne was, if not a Thomist, then at least Thomistic; other recent scholars following Wade have put it thus: "[N]o Platonic account of Traherne's work can make sense of his much neglected Christian Ethicks, which explicates a straightforwardly Aristotelian theory of ethical habituation, as well as a Thomistic account of the perfective nature of the theological virtues."[24] The book you are about to read is a philosophical ethics, but it is also clearly a *theological* ethical treatise too. While these arguments have convinced me of Traherne's rightful place in the Thomistic and the scholastic camp there are other points which will offer a view of Traherne the humanist. For instance, we will see him disputing, apparently *contra* Aquinas, whether theological virtue is infused; but everywhere he offers an argument it reads as disputation from within a tradition rather than from without. And that tradition deals in virtue, but it also deals with the God of Scripture.

In Chapter VII we establish without a doubt that the love which perfects our nature comes from God. This then raises a new question: who is God? What is He like? And, given the tawdry state everything down here is in, what kind of God would create a world that's set up as ours is?

In Chapter VIII we begin to discern the truth, beauty, and goodness of Christianity. And this is discerned through our active lives, yes, but it is known through our intellect's pursuit of truth. A truth that, while indebted to the ancient pagans for certain questions and philosophies, is only ever fully discovered in the gospel, and person, of Jesus Christ.

---

[24] Paul Cefalu, "Thomistic Metaphysics and Ethics in the Poetry and Prose of Thomas Traherne," *Literature and Theology* 16, no. 3 (September 2002): 249.

Reading Traherne in light of Aquinas—reading him as a Thomist, or at the least as someone well versed in Thomas—is not to narrow him down. Thomism is not some mere ideology, like Marxism, that lives or dies with its historical circumstance. Nor is it, like Kantianism, attached to the man who gave it birth and his system of thinking. Rather it is a name for a living tradition of Christian philosophical reflection, itself flexible and adaptable, preceding Aquinas and continuing after him.[25] It took up what it could from those who came before it and it continues into the future by doing the same. And Traherne does not wear his vast learning as a banner to overawe you. He rarely cites. But by gathering you up into the world as he has experienced it, and as his intellect has seen it, he trains you in some of the deepest intellectual currents in the history of mankind, a tradition stretching back hundreds of years before Traherne to Aquinas, and through Aquinas to Augustine and from him to the Greek Fathers, and beyond them to Aristotle, Plato, and Socrates. Traherne's *Ethics* is a profound and beautiful contribution to the Christian tradition of theological-ethical reflection. It should be read as a book that intends to edify you through the renewing of your mind, but also transform you through the re-habituation of your attitudes and behaviors.

---

[25] John Haldane, Timothy Chappell, Dagfinn Follesdal, Bas C. van Fraassen, John Greco, Bonnie Kent, Christopher Martin, et al., "Thomism and the Future of Catholic Philosophy: 1998 Aquinas Lecture," *New Blackfriars* 80, no. 938 (April 1999): 158–213.

Introduction to the Modernization

To my shame I once wrote of a modernization of Thomas Dekker's *Four Birds of Noah's Ark: A Prayerbook from the Time of Shakespeare* by Robert Hudson:

> There is a question standing between you and this modern edition which is: who would read this version of it? I imagine the ideal audience for Dekker to be someone who's into English literature of the sixteenth and seventeenth century. Not casually into it, but really into it. This is the guy who'd corner you at a party to explain why "The Wild Goose Chase" by Fletcher is funnier than "The Isle of Dogs" by Johnson. If you asked this person what version of the bible they read they'd drag out the old Dangerfieldesque saw: "well the authorized version was translated by people who didn't know Greek or Hebrew, but modern translators don't know English...Am-I-Right?!" I could imagine someone like that seeking out to read Dekker's obscure book of prayers. The problem is I can't imagine that person either needing or being at all pleased with the "updated" language provided by Hudson. Wouldn't the slight archaicism be part of the pleasure?[26]

I had no idea then the extent to which God's providence relishes irony. I had only just been hired by the

---

[26] Colin Redemer, "A Review of *Four Birds of Noah's Ark*," *Englewood Review of Books*, January 26, 2018, https://englewoodreview.org/thomas-dekker-four-birds-of-noahs-ark-review/.

Davenant Institute and discovered our extensive "translation" project of classic and important, though sorely neglected, works from the English Reformation. I don't think it was more than a year after my writing this when I was approached by Brad Littlejohn to take up the task you hold before you: a modernization of Thomas Traherne's *Christian Ethics*.

On the matter of the importance and necessity of the modernization projects I have little to add to the prefaces one can find in our edition of *The Laws of Ecclesiastical Polity: Books I–IV*. There, Littlejohn makes the compelling case that, as the education system in the English-speaking world continues to decline and moves farther from ever offering a meditation on ultimate things, there opens up a need for some scholars to become gate builders. The masses don't dislike Dekker, Hooker, or Traherne. The masses have never met them. They've barely been acquainted with Shakespeare, and when they have, they have spat it out like a child's first taste of *époisses*. As the greatest living Anglican writer, Peter Hitchens, put it, "We…live in the ruins of a lost civilization, scuttling in and out of doorways too tall for us."[27] Doorways *too tall* for us. I didn't understand what that meant when I first read it. One must stand in the Emperor's Door in the Hagia Sophia and look at the deep antiquity and splendid vastness and dazzled visitors to get the measure of what Hitchens has in mind. Such doors humble us. It was clearly not made for me, and walking through it is as uncomfortable as wearing clothes tailored for some much

[27] Peter Hitchens, "A Church That Was," *First Things*, May 2016, https://www.firstthings.com/article/2016/05/a-church-that-was.

mightier man. The great works of poetry and philosophy are like that.

And much like at the Hagia Sophia, the visitors who mill about in the great books are mostly ignorant of what they read. Like tourists in Paris who pose endlessly before the Iron Monstrosity, the goal is plainly about the reproduction of the image of what everyone has already seen as opposed to *actually seeing*. In Hagia Sophia when one looks in the eyes of the average tourist one sees no sense of the meaning of the placement of the Emperor's throne relative to the altar and his wife's seat. They amble haphazardly, mostly interested in their upcoming brunch of *simit* and *kahve*. At least across the street at the Blue Mosque there is piety and pilgrimage.

And so, the goal of a modernization is to build the right-sized homely postern which will allow people to approach Traherne and come to know him. Two points then on this.

First, the goal is to remove the distaste for his style of writing. The way of writing shifts over time. What communicated clearly to the reading audience in Traherne's day is not the same as ours. This is a change in writing styles but also a change in readership. While mass literacy as we understand it was still in the future for Traherne, his era was not as illiterate as many of us commonly assume. Our records of the era indicate it is likely that between thirty and sixty percent of the population of England was able to read and write in the seventeenth century. Still, for many of these, due to the cost of books, "literacy" would have meant the ability to read the Bible, pamphlets, and legal documents.[28] Traherne then was aware that his writing was for a small and elite audience, even while he claims in the introduction to the *Christian Ethics* that he is writing for the educated layman.[29] Such educated laymen *were* rare and elite. But the limit was mostly material. Such people as could afford the book had also afforded an education and could afford the leisure which such education required. We come to Traherne on the other side of great change: mass education, mass literacy, efficiency of everything as a goal in opposition to the goal of leisure, a total domination of the world by the dream of equality, as well as the vast reduction in the cost of print production. Because of this, writing and reading have expanded yet simultaneously those same habits have been simplified. Reading Traherne, then, or any writer of his time, given our starting point, is hard. Traherne's style can seem self-indulgent, or even baroque. We tend to write (and read) short sentences of relatively simple construction. And we are also used to a much more highly standardized spelling and punctuation regime, much to some people's chagrin. Therefore, this modernization sets out to smooth the way for readers to engage his writing and make it palatable. It takes the large, unwieldy sentences and breaks them up into smaller bits where possible. It updates archaic language, language that amateur philologists like me find pleasant. At points, we have added to the text itself where we felt Traherne's original sense was simply too obscure,

---

[28] For more on this see David Cressy, "Literacy in Seventeenth-Century England: More Evidence," *The Journal of Interdisciplinary History* 8, no. 1 (Summer 1977): 141–50.

[29] See Carol Marks's introduction to the *Christian Ethicks* (Ithaca: Cornell University Press, 1968).

though we have sought to keep these interventions to a minimum and keep most additional explanations in footnotes. We have also altered Traherne's lengthy chapter headings to be more in keeping with contemporary standards. And of course extensive work has been done standardizing the spelling and grammar to adhere to modern norms. Notably, Traherne's English capitalized nouns making his English visibly closer to its German cousin. In a very few places a sentence or two has been added to make the broken-up sentences fit together logically for the reader. We have also added numbers to each chapter's paragraphs to aid navigation and reference. Any direct quotations from Scripture have been adjusted to fit the American Standard Version, though Traherne tends to simply weave Scripture into his prose rather than quote directly, and we have not generally amended his language in such instances.

A sample of what is to come may be in order here. From the modernization in Chapter IV:

> When we fell into sin, we let death and misery into the world, contracted shame and guilt upon ourselves, defiled our nature with deformities and diseases, and on that occasion made many things necessary to our happiness that were not so before. Insofar as they have both a mixture of bitterness and advantage in them, we may thank ourselves for the bitterness, and God for the advantage. For as by sin we forfeited our happiness, so a new obedience consisting in the practice of proper virtues was necessary to recover it. These virtues, whose names and natures were different in kind from those virtues

which were natural to us in Eden. These were virtues we had never heard of before; all which we must look upon, not as food, but medicine. As we are now sin-sick we consider them under the notion of remedies; we do not focus on the bitter taste of medicine but the health it brings, and so we do not get surprised that there should be something in these new virtues that is distasteful to sense. They are now, once we know them and place them in their context, infinitely agreeable to reason (p.45).

Compare to Traherne's original:

WHEN we fell into Sin, we let Death and Misery into the World, contracted shame and guilt upon our selves, defiled our Nature with Deformities and Diseases, and made many Things upon that Occasion, necessary to our Happiness, that before were not so: And whereas they have a Mixture of *Bitterness* and *Advantage* in them, we may thank our selves for the *Bitterness*, and GOD for the *Advantage*: For as we, by Sin forfeited our *Happiness*, so a new Obedience, consisting in the practice of proper Vertues, was necessary to recover it. Vertues, whose Names and Natures were of another kind, and never heard of before: All which we must look upon, not as Food, but Physick, and considering them under the notion of Remedies, not admire that there should be something in them Distasteful to Sence, tho they are now, when their Occasions are known, infinitely agreeable to Reason.

Traherne was a poet in his own right and to do too much changing of his language feels something close to a sin. As I say above, the goal was to make his own style approachable for the average layperson to read with ease and enjoyment.

Second, the goal of all of this is not just to have us read him but to help us see Traherne and to see the world through him—to see as he saw. As Lewis might have put it: Traherne isn't a man looking at the beam of light thrown off by theology—aloof, scientific, and technical. Rather, he is enraptured, looking along it, warming his intellect directly in the light of the countenance of God.[30] All of philosophy is an ever-greater attempt to see reality for the sheer delight which seeing it has to offer. The motive for building this postern which you hold, this portal into the seventeenth century, is that more people might put out of mind for a moment their ever growing distractions and see as Traherne saw. For all his rarified language and the elite nature of his audience, he in fact does have so much to offer any Christian. I hope, in putting this book out, to add my small drop to the growing sea of work on Traherne so that he will not be forgotten, and additionally that in reading this book more of us begin to see our lives as he saw his: with deep gratitude and joy and a hope for the more that is still to come.

The goal of the modernizer's art is the same as that of the expert teacher: to equip the pupil for his absence. Where this modernization has made Traherne and his vision more visible to you, let us thank both Traherne and the divine *Logos*. Where you see the art of the modernization, I

---

[30] C. S. Lewis, "Meditation in a Toolshed," in *God in the Dock* (Grand Rapids, MI: Eerdmans, 1970), 212–15.

apologize in advance, for it is precisely there where I have failed. At the least, God willing, this work will move a few more people to embark on the very long, never easy, but always fruitful work of educating oneself—of endeavoring to grow into a man worthy of standing in the threshold of the great temples.

TO THE READER

THE GOAL of this work is not to entertain you, but to elevate your soul, to refine your soul's understanding, inform its judgment, and polish it for conversation. To purify and enflame the heart, to enrich the mind, and to guide men (that stand in need of help) in the way of virtue. And it will do this not by fasting with a long face but by exciting men's desire, encouraging them to travel, comforting them in the journey, and so at last to lead them to true happiness, both here and after death.[1]

I do not need to write about virtues in the ordinary way, as they are duties enjoined by God's law; the author of *The Whole Duty of Man* has done this excellently already.[2] Nor

---

[1] The word "happiness" here and throughout the text is "felicity" in Traherne's original. His usage is well known and would have been more common in his era. As the text will show, he means something more profound by it than we tend to encounter in everyday modern usage. But that difference would have been the same in the original usage of "felicity." There has never been a generation where the public was made up of philosophers. For a parallel example consider the meaning Aristotle has in his usage of εὐδαιμονία, which is generally translated as "happiness," in the *Nicomachean Ethics*.

[2] *The Whole Duty of Man* is a devotional book published anonymously in 1658 with an introduction by Henry Hammond. The principal authorship of it, however, has been debated since its publication. It was likely anonymous because of the precarious

do I need to write about them as prudential expedients and means for a man's peace and honor on earth; that was in some measure done by the Frenchman Charron in *Of Wisdome*.[3] My purpose is to satisfy the curious and unbelieving soul concerning the reality, force, and efficacy of virtue. And, having some advantages from the knowledge I gained of the nature of happiness (by many years of earnest and diligent study), my business is to make as visible as possible the luster of its beauty, dignity, and glory. This is accomplished by showing how necessary virtue is as the means to happiness: how sweet, how full of reason, how desirable in itself, how just and amiable, how delightful, and how powerfully conducive also to glory. Just consider how naturally virtue carries us to the temple of bliss, and how immeasurably transcendent it is in all kinds of excellency.

Also (if I may speak freely), my office is to carry and enhance virtue to its utmost height, to open its beauty, and to make the glory of God appear in the blessedness of man, by setting forth its infinite excellence. This will be accomplished by taking out of the treasuries of humanity those arguments that will display the great perfection of the

---

nature of high-church Anglicanism in the interregnum period in which it came out. Modern scholarly consensus is that it was written by Richard Allestree.

[3] This is a reference to the sixteenth-century French philosopher and theologian Pierre Charron (1541–1603). The italics here are mine. Traherne is advocating his readers to consult the text *Of Wisdome*, which was a translation of a selection of Charron's work carried out by Samson Lennard in 1612. It is possible that Traherne was acquainted with the various original works in the French. If so, it shows particular broadmindedness for Traherne to invite readers to consult Charron, a Roman Catholic who argued against Protestantism, and who (as a skeptic) was also accused of atheism.

end of man, which he may achieve by the capacity of his nature, and by opening the nature of virtue itself, thereby to display the marvelous beauty of religion, and light the soul to the sight of its perfection.

I do not speak much of vice, which is a far easier theme, because I am entirely taken up with the abundance of worth and beauty in virtue. I have so much to say of the positive and intrinsic goodness of its nature. But besides, since a straight line is the measure both of itself and of a crooked one, I conclude that the very glory of virtue, well understood, will make all vice appear like dirt before a jewel when they are compared together. No, as soon as vice is named in the presence of these virtues, it will look like poison and a contagion or, if you will, as black as malice and ingratitude. There need be no other exposition of its nature to exhort and dissuade men from the love of it than the illustration of its contrary.

Virtues are listed in the rank of invisible things. Some are so blind as to deny there are any at all. Yet it may (and will be) made apparent that all the peace and beauty in the world proceeds from these invisible things. Similarly, all honor and security are founded in them, all glory and esteem are acquired by them. For the prosperity of all kingdoms is laid in the goodness of God and of men. Were there nothing in the world but the works of friendship, which proceed from the highest virtue, they alone would testify of its excellency.[4] For there can be no safety where there is any

---

[4] The word "friendship" in this sentence was "amity" in the original. In other places in the text I have substituted "goodwill," but those who are familiar with Aristotle's writings might also consider these words in the sense which is often captured by the

treachery; but were all truth and courtesy exercised with fidelity and love there could be no injustice or complaint in the world, no strife or violence. In such a world all would be bounty, joy, and complacency. Were there no blindness, every soul would be full of light, and the face of happiness be seen, and the earth be turned into heaven.

The things we discuss here are great and mighty. They touch the essence of every soul and are of infinite concern because the happiness acquired by them is eternal. I do not mean immortal only, but worthy of eternity. And it is impossible to be happy without them. We explain man's great and sovereign end, the nature of blessedness, and the means to attain it. We explain knowledge and love, wisdom and goodness, righteousness and holiness, justice and mercy, prudence and courage, temperance and patience, meekness and humility, contentment, magnanimity and modesty, liberality and magnificence, the ways by which love is begotten in the soul, gratitude, faith, hope, and charity, repentance, devotion, fidelity, and godliness. In all, we show what sublime and mysterious creatures virtues are, which depend upon the operations of man's soul. We show their great extent, their use and value, their origin and their end, their objects and their times. Which virtues belong to the estate of innocence, which to the estate of misery and grace, and which to the estate of glory? Which ones are the food of the soul, and the works of nature? Which were occasioned by sin as medicines and expedients only? Which are essential to happiness, and which are accidental? Which time-bound, and which eternal? We also treat the true reason of their imposition, why they all are commanded, and

---

translation "concord." "General friendliness with one's fellows" is the overall sense. Sometimes "political friendship."

how wise and gracious God is in enjoining them. It is by this means that all atheism is put to flight, and all unfaithfulness: the soul is reconciled to the Lawgiver of the world and taught to delight in his commandments. All enmity and discontentment must vanish as clouds and darkness before the sun when the beauty of virtue appears in its brightness and glory. It is impossible that the splendor of its nature should be seen without all religion and happiness being made manifest.

Perhaps you will learn some new ideas. Yet when they are examined, I hope it will appear to the reader that it was the actual knowledge of true happiness that taught me to speak of virtue. And, moreover, that there is not the least bit pertaining to the catholic faith that is contradicted or altered in my work. For I firmly retain all that was established in the ancient councils—and see cause to do so—even in the highest and most transcendent mysteries.[5] But I enrich all, by farther opening the grandeur and glory of religion, with the interior depths and beauties of faith.

---

[5] Traherne here presumably refers to at least the first four ecumenical councils of Nicaea, Constantinople, Ephesus, and Chalcedon. He should be read with the backdrop of the seventeenth-century Church of England in mind. The 39 Articles contain two useful articles on the issue of what constitutes a council and how those relate to our faith. Article 20 clarifies that the supreme authority of the Church is Scripture. The Church is beneath Scripture, not above it, nor equal to it, but subject to and accountable to it. Article 21 states that general councils have to be called by the rightful authority (outlawing, for example, Trent), that they can and have erred (such as Lateran I's requirement of clerical celibacy), and that they, like the Church, only have authority wherein they point to and rearticulate the truths found in Scripture. The truth of the Word of God is the basis for retaining that which is established in "ancient councils."

Yet indeed it is not I, but God that has enriched the nature of it. I only bring the wealth of virtue to light, which the infinite wisdom, goodness, and power of God have seated there. Though learned men know perhaps far better than I, yet I humbly crave pardon for casting in my *widow's mite*. I have really one thing to say: the glory of God and the sublime perfection of human nature, are united in virtue. By virtue, the creation is made useful and the universe delightful. All the works of God are crowned with their end by the glory of virtue. For whatever is good and profitable for men is made sacred because it is delightful and well-pleasing to God. God, being love by nature, delights in his creatures' welfare.

There are two sorts of actions necessary to bliss that must work together—actions in God and actions in men, and actions too in all the creatures. The sun must warm, but it must not burn. The earth must bring forth, but not swallow up. The air must cool without starving, and the sea moisten without drowning. Meats must feed but not poison. Rain must fall, but not oppress. Thus, in the inferior creatures you see that actions are of several kinds. But these may be reduced to the actions of God, from whom they spring. For he prepares all these creatures for us. And it is necessary to the happiness of his sons that he should make all things healing and amiable, not odious and destructive; that he should love, and not hate. And the actions of men must fit with these of God, and his creatures. They must not despise blessings because they are given, but esteem them; not trample them under feet, because they have the benefit of them, but magnify and extol them. They too must love, and not hate. They must not kill and murder but serve and please one another. They must not scorn great and inestimable gifts, because they are common, for so the angels would lose all the happiness of heaven. If God should do the most great and glorious things that infinite wisdom could devise, but men resolve to be blind, and perverse, and senseless, then all will be in vain; the most high and sacred things will increase their misery. This may give you some little glimpse of the excellency of virtue.

You may easily discern that my design is to reconcile men to God and make them fit to delight in him. My last end is to celebrate his praises, in communion with the angels. In this I beg the agreement of the reader, for we can never praise him enough, nor be fit enough to praise him. No other man (at least) can make us so without our own willingness and endeavor to do it.

Above all, pray to be sensitive to the excellence of the creation, for upon the due sense of its excellence the life of happiness wholly depends. Pray to be sensitive to the excellence of divine laws, and to all the goodness which your soul comprehends. Desire a lively sense of all you know, of the excellence of God and of eternal love, of your own excellence, and of the worth and value of all things altogether. For to *feel* is as necessary as to see their glory.

I:
THE END OF VIRTUE

1. IT IS the prerogative of human nature to understand itself, and to guide its operations to a known end. This end is forfeit if one lives at random, without considering what is worthy of his endeavors, or fit for his desires.[1]

2. The end is that which crowns the work. This goal inspires the soul with desire, and desire gives rise to a quick and vigorous industry. It is achieved last, but conceived first, in every operation. All means which can be used in the acquisition of it derive their value from its excellence. We are encouraged to use these means only on the account of that end which is reached by them.

3. It is the purpose of moral instruction to teach men the nature of virtue, and to encourage them in the practice of it, by explaining its use and efficacy.

4. The excellence of virtue is what makes it both necessary to happiness and able also to produce it. Its excellence consists in this: virtue is the only means by which happiness can be obtained.

---

[1] "End" here and throughout is used as in the ancient Greek sense of *telos*: the ultimate aim or "final cause" of something.

5. Since consideration of the end is what animates us to the use of the means, whoever deals with virtue is right to put the end at the beginning. And further, they should first show the excellence of bliss before they open the nature of virtue. It is a vain thing to discover the means unless the end is desired. Otherwise, no matter how often we are taught or commended to be virtuous, it will have no effect—like a man with wood, a hammer, and nails but no desire to build. For if we despise the end, all our activity is fruitless. It may at best instruct us in the means, but such knowledge is vain. It will produce no good effect in us.

6. Reason is the faculty by which man is able to contemplate his end. It is a singular advantage that privileges him above the beasts. It enables him not only to examine the nature and perfection of his end, but also the justness and fitness of the means used to achieve the end. It also allows him to examine the singular excellence of his first cause, as its glory and goodness appears in his design and contrivance; especially in making man's happiness so complete and perfect.

7. The heathens, who invented the name of "ethics," fell very short in the knowledge of man's end; but they are worse than heathens who never consider it.[2]

---

[2] "Heathens" inventing "the name of ethics" is not intended as an insult but rather as a straightforward way of identifying the paternity of the language and the tradition of thinking in which Traherne is engaging. Ethics, in the Greek ἠθικός and pronounced *ethicos*, means "pertaining to character." The study of human character, its development and its possible malformations, was initially undertaken in ancient Greece among pagan philosophers—most notably Socrates, Plato, and Aristotle. The

8. The more excellent the end is, the more prone by nature we are to pursue it, and all the means conducive in getting us there are the more desirable.

9. Reason, which is the formal essence of the soul of man, guides him to desire those things which are absolutely supreme.[3] For it is an eternal property in reason to prefer the better above the worse. He who prefers the worse above the better acts against nature, and swerves from the rule of right reason.

10. Whatever varieties of opinion there are concerning happiness, all conclude and agree in this, that man's ultimate purpose is his perfect happiness. And the more excellent his happiness is, the more ought his soul to be enflamed with the desire of it and inspired with the greater industry.

11. The more perfect his bliss is, the greater is man's crime of despising it. To pursue an infinite and eternal happiness

---

systematic study of character was their best guess as to what "the Good" as applied to "the human" would be. Jews needed no such study as they had much more immediate access to the law. Obedience to the law, as conceptualized in terms of ethics, came later as humans reflected on the meaning of the Torah.

[3] "Essence" is a traditional philosophical way of asking about "the whatness" of any given thing. What is it that makes such and such a thing the thing that it is? The use of the term "Form" modifies this slightly to clarify that it is not looking for the essence of a particular being but what is it about the type of being that makes it that type. Form, as related to the beings in question, is distinguished from matter and their "material essence." The formal essence of man has been thought to be our rationality combined with our animality at least as far back as Aristotle, even if he didn't use this exact terminology.

is divine and angelic. To pursue an earthly and sensual happiness is brutish. But to place happiness in anger and envy is demonic: the pleasures of malice are bitter and destructive.

12. To live by accident, and never to pursue any happiness at all is neither angelic, nor brutish, nor demonic, but worse than anything in some respect. It is to act against that which makes us human, and to wage war with our very selves. They who place their ease in carelessness are of all others the greatest enemies and disturbers of themselves.

13. It is madness and folly to pursue the first object that presents itself without a clear idea of happiness. And those who suspect that there is no true happiness and therefore content themselves in the enjoyment of low things are pitiable. Such people are common. The disputations concerning the nature of happiness argue its existence.[4] And we must cease to be men before we can extinguish the desire of being happy. He only is truly generous who aspires to the most perfect blessedness of which God and nature have made him capable.

14. There is great danger in choosing our happiness. And the greater the danger, the greater the watch we should set over our own minds lest we should be seduced and

---

[4] Traherne's point in this sentence is that all the great philosophical disputations on happiness (e.g., Aristotle's *Nicomachean Ethics* or, less clearly, Plato's *Phaedo*) argue affirmatively for its existence. Arguments against the existence of happiness have no philosophical pedigree. And those who might argue that happiness (or truth) doesn't exist must always be asked, "Then why are you still arguing?" Those who eat dirt still *eat*.

deceived. Just look at how eager men are in their disputations concerning happiness—this proves the weight of the nature of the theme being examined.

15. Hastiness in grasping an unexamined happiness is the great occasion of all the error about it among the vulgar. They are led, like beasts, by their sense and appetite, without discerning or improving any other faculty. The lip of the cup is anointed with honey, which, as soon as they taste, they drink it up, though the liquor is nothing but gall and poison. They are deluded with a show: instead of pleasure, they rush headlong to their own destruction.

16. It is as natural for man to desire happiness as to live and breathe. Sense and instinct carry him to happiness, as well as reason. Only reason should rectify and direct his instinct, inform his sense, and complete his essence by inducing those perfections of which it is capable.

17. Things good in themselves, when they attempt to supplant better things, can become evil. Better things are evil if preferred to the best. This is especially true where the choice of the one hinders the acquisition of the other. For where good, better, and best, are subservient to each other, the one is the better for the others' sake. But where they interfere and oppose each other, the good are bad in comparison to the better, and the better worse than the best. This is why reason cannot assent to any happiness less than the supreme. Such a happiness must be infinite, because the almighty power which made reason active is limitless in its operations. It never rests, except in the production of a glorious act that is infinite in perfection.

18. If happiness is infinite, the loss of happiness is as great. The misery of missing our happiness is intolerable. For (our eyes being open) a loss that is incomprehensible must produce a grief unmeasurable, an anguish as infinite as our damage.

19. Inferior happinesses are but miseries compared with the highest. A penny is good and pleases a beggar in need, but a gold coin is better. An estate of ten thousand pounds a year is better than a gold coin, but our ambition carries us to principalities and empires. An empire is more desirable than a province, and the wider, the richer, the better it is, the more desirable. But the empire of all the earth is a bubble compared to the heavens, and the heavens themselves are less than nothing compared to an infinite dominion.

20. Perfect happiness is not dominion, nor pleasure, nor riches alone, nor learning, nor virtue, nor honor; but all these in perfection. It requires that every soul should be capable of infinite dominion, pleasure, learning, and honor for the full and perfect attainment of it.

21. If all these are infinite and eternal in that happiness which is prepared for man, those actions are of inestimable value by virtue of which his happiness is gained. And it becomes his wisdom and courage to suffer many things for so noble an end, especially if it may in any measure be thereby acquired and enjoyed in this life.

22. The great reason why God has concealed happiness from the knowledge of man is the enhancement of its nature

and value. But that which most conceals it is the corruption of nature. For as we have corrupted, so have we blinded ourselves. Yet we are led by instinct to eagerly thirst after things unknown, remote, and forbidden. The truth is, our palates are spoiled, and our digestion so corrupted that until our nature is purified by a little work, to make happiness known is to expose it to contempt and censure. Happiness is too great and pure for perverted nature.

23. The concealment of an object whets our appetite, and puts an edge upon our endeavors, and this carries a mystery in it. For whereas the maxim is *ignoti nulla cupido*, all love comes in at the eye. [5] We desire an object to which we are blind, and the more blind we are, the more restless. We are touched by an unknown beauty which we never saw, and in the midst of our ignorance are actuated with a tendency which does not abate the value of our virtues, but puts life and energy into our actions.

24. Though highest happiness cannot be perfectly understood (because it is incomprehensible to men on earth), yet we may discern a great deal about it. What we can come to know will serve to meet our instinct, feed our capacity, animate our endeavor, encourage our expectation (to hope for more than we enjoy), enable us to subdue our lusts, support us in temptations, and assist us in overcoming all obstacles.

25. Even if happiness were no more than infinite honors and pleasures, that would be enough to allure us. But the

---

[5] "There is no desire for what is unknown," or "ignorance is bliss."

idea of a happy ending—the idea that all things can conclude in the best of manners, in communion with God, being full of life, and beauty, and perfection in himself, and having the certain assurance that all will be included in his bliss—this thought is a thing so divine that the very hope of it fills us with comfort here, and to see it realized will be perfect satisfaction hereafter.

26. He that can enjoy all things in the image of God does not need to covet their enjoyment in a baser manner: man was made in God's image that he might live in his likeness.

27. I am not so stoic as to make all happiness consist in mere apathy. Freedom from passion is not the solution, nor is it to give the passions all their liberty. Neither do I persuade you to renounce the advantages of wealth and honor any more than those of beauty and wit. For as a man may be happy without all these, so may he make a happy use of them when he has them. He may be happy with difficulty without them, but easily with them. If not in heaven, yet certainly on earth, the goods of fortune concur to the completion of time-bound happiness, and therefore where they are freely given, they are not to be despised.

28. That which I desire to teach a man is how to make a good use of all the advantages of his birth and breeding. How, in the increase of riches and honors, to be happy in their enjoyment. How to secure himself in the temptations of affluence, and to make a man glorious in himself, and delightful to others in abundance. Or else, if affliction should arise, and the state of affairs change, I would teach how to triumph over adverse fortune, and to be happy

notwithstanding his calamities and how to govern himself in all estates so as to turn them to his own advantage.

29. For though happiness is not absolutely perfect in this world, nor so complete in poverty, as in a great and plentiful estate; you are not to believe that wealth is absolutely necessary. Sometimes it is required to forfeit all for the sake of happiness. Nothing is absolutely necessary to bliss but grace and virtue, though to perfect bliss, ease and honor are absolutely necessary.

30. There are many degrees of blessedness beneath the most supreme. They all are transcendently sweet and delightful. And it sometimes happens that what is most bitter to sense is pleasant to reason.

31. Rather than make shipwreck of a good conscience, we must do as mariners in a storm, and cast our riches overboard for our own preservation. It is better to lose them than ourselves.

32. Virtue is desirable and glorious, because it teaches us through many difficulties in this tempestuous world to sail smoothly, and attain the haven.

II:
THE NATURE OF HAPPINESS

1. ARISTOTLE and his school, so far as they contemplated the nature and estate of man in this world, were wise.[1] They defined the goods of the body, soul, and fortune as each and all necessary for man's perfect happiness. For difficulties and conflicts are not essential to the nature of bliss nor consistent with the enjoyment of its fullness and perfection.

2. There is the way and the journey's end.

3. On the way to happiness many things are to be endured that are not to be desired. And, therefore, it is necessary to make a distinction between the way to happiness and the rest which we attain at the end of our journey.

4. The goods of the soul are absolutely necessary in the way to happiness; the goods of the body are very fitting, and those of fortune are comfort enough. But the latter of these are not to be pursued with too much eagerness.

---

[1] The text originally read "The peripatetics" instead of "Aristotle and his school" here, and has been clarified for readers less familiar with the history of Greek philosophy.

5. The goods of the soul are wisdom, knowledge, courage, all the virtues, all the passions, affections, powers, and faculties. And these you know are absolutely necessary.

6. The goods of the body are health, agility, beauty, vivacity, strength, and liberty. And these shall be enjoyed in heaven itself, together with those of the soul. By this you may discern that the goods of the body are real parts and ingredients of happiness.

7. The goods of fortune are food and clothing, houses and lands, riches, honors, relations and friends, with all those fitting circumstances outside of the body that are subject to chance. By these virtue is assisted, and a noble use may be made of them in works of justice, hospitality, courtesy, and charity, which may redound to our greater happiness here and in heaven.

8. The more honor and pleasure we enjoy, the greater and more perfect is our present happiness, though many times in the way to happiness we are forced to quit all these for the preservation of our innocence.

9. Brave resolve in fleeing all transitory things for the preservation of our virtue is more conducive to our future perfection than the greatest ease imaginable in our present condition.

10. It is incumbent upon us, as a special part of our care, to take heed that we are not ensnared by the easiness of prosperity. This is the mistake of setting up our rest on the way to happiness. Nor should we deceive ourselves in

thinking the goods of fortune to be essential. Nor should we discourage ourselves by thinking it impossible to be happy without them. Our thoughts and affections must be always disentangled, that we may run, briskly, the race set before us, and close with sublime perfection of bliss, as our only portion and desire.

11. Happiness is rightly defined as the perfect enjoyment of a perfect soul acting in perfect life by perfect virtue. For the attainment of this perfection, we must, in the way to happiness, endure all afflictions that can befall us. For though they are not parts of happiness themselves, yet we may acknowledge them as great advantages for the exercise of virtue and reckon our calamities among our joys when we bear and overcome them in a virtuous manner, because they add to our honor, and contribute much to our perfection, both here, and hereafter.

12. For this purpose, we are to remember that our present condition is not that of reward, but labor. Ours is an estate of trial, not of enjoyment. Our condition is that we are to toil, and sweat, and work hard for the promised wages; an appointed seed time for a future harvest; a real warfare to gain a glorious victory. Warriors in such a battle must expect some blows, and delight in the hazards and encounters we meet with because they will be crowned with a glorious and joyful triumph and be attended with ornaments and trophies far surpassing the bare tranquility of idle peace.

13. When we can cheerfully look on an army of misfortunes without dismay, we may then freely and delightfully contemplate the nature of the highest happiness.

14. Aristotle never heard of our ascension into heaven, nor of sitting down in the throne of God, yet by a lucky hit (if I may so say) discovered upon the nature of blessedness. For a perfect enjoyment by perfect virtue is all that can be thought of: it implies our objective and our formal happiness.[2]

15. Objective happiness is all the goodness that is fit to be enjoyed either in God or in his creatures. Formal happiness is an active enjoyment of all objects by contemplation and love, attended with uncritical satisfaction in all their perfections.

16. Perfect enjoyment implies the perfection of all its objects. Among which God himself is one, angels and saints are next, the world also with all the variety of creatures in it. So too the laws of God, his ways in all ages, and his eternal counsels and divine attributes are other objects of our

---

[2] Aristotle's theory was that happiness was an activity of the soul in accordance with virtue; and where there is more than one virtue, with the greatest of them. Our soul is that of rational animals. And virtue (whether moral or intellectual) is only virtue *when we take pleasure in its activation*. This final point is key: "being good" and "enjoying life" were not to ever be at odds in human life, unless it is so because the human is attempting to grow out of a habituated defect. In other words humans cannot ever be good until they enjoy the goodness they are being. The ultimate happiness then is *to be as God* and for humans to have this goal actualized would be supremely *enjoyable*. Traherne, as other have before and since, marveled at Aristotle's ability to formulate a fitting solution to the puzzle of being human and to do so without access to special revelation. For more on our enjoyment of God, compare *The Westminster Catechism* Question 1 with I.II.I of Aquinas's *Summa*, addressing "Man's Last End."

content and pleasure. Unless all these are perfect in their nature, variety, number, extent, relation, use, and value, our enjoyment cannot be simply perfect. A greater and more perfect enjoyment might, upon the production of better objects, be contrived. No enjoyment can be truly perfect that is not conversant about the highest things. The more beautiful the object is, the more pleasant is the enjoyment. But where delight may be increased, the enjoyment is imperfect.

17. A perfect soul is a transcendent mystery. Just as God could not be perfect if it were possible for any essence to be better than he, in the same way the soul, God's image, would not be perfect could any more perfect soul be created.

18. A perfect soul is a soul in which no defect or blemish can be discerned. It is perfect in the variety and number of its powers, in the fitness and measure of every power, in the use and value of every endowment. A perfect soul is that to which nothing can be added to please our desire. As all its objects are perfect, so it is itself. It is able to see all that is to be seen, to love all that is lovely, to hate all that is hateful, to desire all that is desirable, to honor all that is honorable, to esteem all that can be valued, to delight in all that is delightful, and to enjoy all that is good and fit to be enjoyed. If its power did fall short of any one object, or of any one perfection in any object, or of any degree in any perfection, it would be imperfect; it would not be the masterpiece of eternal power.

19. Perfect life is the full exertion of perfect ability. It implies two things: perfection of vigor and perfection of

intelligence. Thus, we need an activity of life, reaching through all immensity, to all objects whatsoever and a freedom from all dullness in understanding. For the intellect, we need an exquisite tenderness of perception in feeling even the least object. For the execution of perfect vigor, we need a sphere of activity that runs parallel with the omnipresence of the Godhead. For if any soul lives so imperfectly as to see and know only some objects, or to love them indistinctly, and less than they deserve, its life is imperfect. Either it is remiss, or despite being fervent, it is nevertheless confined.

20. Perfect enjoyment (as it implies the perfection of all objects) more nearly imports the intrinsic perfection of its own operations. For if its objects are perfect in themselves but the soul does not sense their excellence, a blemish lies upon the enjoyment. If the enjoyment of one object be lost, or one degree of the enjoyment abated, it is imperfect.

21. Perfect virtue may best be understood by a consideration of its particulars. Perfect knowledge is a thorough and complete understanding of all that may be known. Perfect righteousness is a full and adequate esteem of all the value that is in things. It is a kind of spiritual justice, whereby we do right to ourselves and to all other beings. If we render to any object less than it deserves, we are not just toward it. Perfect wisdom is that whereby we choose a most perfect end, actually pursue it by most perfect means, and acquire and enjoy it in the most perfect manner. If we aim at an inferior end, our wisdom is imperfect; and so it is if we pursue it by feeble and inferior means, or neglect any one of

those advantages whereby we may attain it. And the same may be said of all the virtues.

22. Now, if all objects are infinitely glorious, and all worlds fit to be enjoyed, if God has filled heaven and earth and all the spaces above the heavens with innumerable pleasures, if his infinite wisdom, goodness, and power be fully glorified in every being and the soul be created to enjoy all these in most perfect manner, we may well conclude with the holy Apostle that we are the children of God. And if children, then heirs, heirs of God, and joint heirs with Christ, if so it be that we suffer with him, that we may also be glorified together. Our light affliction, that is but for a moment, works out for us a far more exceeding and eternal weight of glory [Rom. 8:16–18]. Beholding as in a glass the glory of the Lord [1 Cor. 13:12], we shall at last be transformed into the same image from glory to glory, even as by the Spirit of the Lord [2 Cor. 3:12–18]. For all his works, of which the Psalmist speaks, are worthy to be had in remembrance, and are sought out by all those that have pleasure therein [Ps. 111:4]. They are like a mirror, wherein his glory appears as the face of the sun does in a clear fountain. We may conclude further that virtue, by force of which we attain so great a kingdom, is infinitely better than rubies. All the things you can desire are not to be compared to her [Prov. 3:15]. So that with unspeakable comfort we may take courage to go on, not only in the study, but in the practice of all the virtues, concerning which we are to treat in the ensuing pages. For as the Apostle Peter tells us, he has given to us all things that pertain to life and godliness through the knowledge of him that has called us to glory and virtue, through which we are given exceeding great and precious

promises. That by these you might be partakers of the divine nature, having escaped the corruption that is in the world through listlessness. And besides this, says he, giving all diligence, add to your faith, virtue; and to virtue, knowledge; and to knowledge, temperance; and to temperance, patience; and to patience, godliness; and to godliness, brotherly kindness; and to brotherly kindness, charity. In this way you will be abundantly welcomed into the everlasting kingdom of our Lord and Savior Jesus Christ [2 Pet. 1:3–11], whose kingdom being so divine and glorious as it is, we have need to bow our knees to the God and Father of our Lord Jesus Christ, of whom the whole family in heaven and earth is named, that he would grant us according to the riches of his glory to be strengthened with might, by his spirit in the inward man, that Christ may dwell in our hearts by faith, that we being rooted and grounded in love, may be able to comprehend with all saints what is the breadth, and length, and depth, and height, and to know the love of Christ which surpasses knowledge, that we may be filled with all the fullness of God [Eph. 3:14–19].

23. To be partaker of the divine nature, to be filled with all the fullness of God, to enter into his kingdom and glory, to be transformed into his image and made an heir of God and a joint heir with Christ, to live in union and communion with God, and to be made a temple of the Holy Ghost— these are divine and transcendent things that accompany our souls in the perfection of their bliss and happiness. These are the hope and belief of all who are justified, and they are made apparent by the explanation of the very nature of the soul, its inclinations and capacities, the reality and greatness of those virtues of which we are capable, and all

those objects which the universe affords to our contemplation.

III:
VIRTUE DEFINED

1. BEFORE we come to treat particular virtues, it is very fitting that we speak of virtue in general.

2. Virtue is a comprehensive word, which by explaining we shall make the way to the right understanding of all the particular virtues into which it is divided easier. Because the nature of virtue enters into knowledge, faith, hope, charity, prudence, courage, meekness, humility, temperance, justice, liberality, etc., every one of these has its essence opened in part by the explanation of that which enters its nature, that is virtue in general.

3. The category of quality contains within it either natural dispositions or habits; habits may be either virtuous or vicious.[1] Virtuous habits are either theological, intellectual,

---

[1] "The category of quality" here was initially "predicament of quality," which is a very odd phrase to us indeed. While I have not left it in, I flag it for a very particular reason: it supports my thesis from the introduction that Traherne is self-awarely dealing with the Thomistic tradition. This is an oblique (to us) reference to Aristotle's *Categories*, Book VIII, where Aristotle discusses what he means by "quality." The term predicament here is being used to mean "that which can be predicated of," not "difficult situation." "Predication" would perhaps be a more fitting term to modern

moral, or divine, and these are branched into the following kinds of virtue.

4. The theological virtues are generally divided into three: faith, hope, and charity. These are called theological because they have God for their principal object and are, in a peculiar manner, taught by his Word among the mysteries of religion. We may add repentance to these because this virtue, although it be occasioned by sin, is chiefly taught by the Word of God, and respects God as its principal object. On account of this, we shall number the theological virtues to be four: faith, hope, charity, and repentance. We may also add obedience, devotion, and godliness.

5. The intellectual virtues are generally reckoned to be five: intelligence, wisdom, science, prudence, and art. Because the distinction between them is overly particular and curious (at least too obscure for ordinary understanding) we shall reduce them perhaps to a fewer number.

6. Intelligence is the knowledge of principles; science the knowledge of conclusions. Wisdom, that knowledge which results from the union of both prudence and art, has been

---

ears, but "predicament" has a pedigree in the tradition, and so it makes sense to retain its usage so as to place ourselves clearly within said tradition. The Aristotelian term "category" gets translated into Latin by Boethius as "predicament." Quality is one of Aristotle's ten categories, and the Latin Thomistic tradition of the fifteenth to seventeenth centuries often used the term "predicament of quality," not "category of quality." See also John of St. Thomas's *Cursus Philosophicus Thomisticus* and Thomas Cajetan's *Commentary on Aristotle's Categories* in their investigations of the same.

explained poorly and is dimly grasped. The objects of wisdom are always stable. Prudence is that knowledge by which we guide ourselves in thorny and uncertain affairs. Art is that habit by which we are assisted in composing tracts and systems, rather than in regulating our lives. It more frequently appears in fiddling and dancing than in noble deeds. Were it not useful in teachers for the instruction of others, we should scarcely reckon it in the number of virtues.

7. All these are called intellectual virtues, because they are seated in the understanding and chiefly exercised in contemplation. The virtues that are brought down into action are called practical, and at other times moral, because they help us in perfecting our manners, as they relate to our conversation with men.[2]

8. The moral virtues are either principal, or less principal. The principal are four: prudence, justice, temperance, and fortitude. These, because they are the hinges upon which our whole lives turn, are called cardinal and are commonly known by the name of the four cardinal virtues.[3] They are called principal, not only because they are the chief of all moral virtues, but because they enter into every virtue as the four elements of which it is compounded.

9. The less principal virtues are magnificence and liberality, modesty and magnanimity, gentleness of behavior, affability, courtesy, truth, and urbanity. These are called less

---

[2] Traherne's note here: "Manners in Latin are called *mores* whence the English word moral is derived."

[3] Traherne's note here: "*cardo* is a hinge."

principal, not because they are indifferent, or may be accounted useless, for then they would not be virtues. Rather, they are called less principal because, though their practice is of extraordinary importance in their places, they are more remote and help us less on the way to happiness and are more confined in their operations.

10. Divine virtues (which we put instead of the pagan heroic ones) are such as have God not only for their object and end, but their pattern and example. They are virtues which are seen in his eternal life. By practicing them we also are changed into the same image and are made partakers of the divine knowledge and truth. In the most sublime height, we confess them to be three, but we shall chiefly insist upon goodness, righteousness, and holiness. All of these will appear in divine love which, in a more peculiar manner, will be handled later.

11. Besides all these, there are some virtues which may more properly be called Christian, because they are nowhere else taught but in the Christian religion, they are founded on the love of Christ, and they are the only virtues distinguishing a Christian from the rest of the world. These include showing love to enemies, meekness, and humility.

12. All these virtues are found under one common head, because they meet in one common nature which bears the name of virtue. The essence of this being well understood will lead to the clear knowledge of each one in particular.

13. Virtue (in general) is that habit of soul by force of which we attain our happiness. Or, if you please, it is a right and

well-ordered habit of mind which facilitates the soul in all its operations, ordering it to blessedness. These terms are to be unfolded.

14. (1) Virtue is a habit, and all habits are either acquired or infused. By calling it a habit, we distinguish it from a natural disposition or a power of the soul. For a natural disposition is an innate inclination which attended our birth and began with our beings; it is one not chosen by our wills, nor acquired by industry. These dispositions, because they do not flow from our choice and industry, cannot be accounted as virtues. It's true indeed that virtuous habits are sometimes infused in a miraculous manner, but then they are rather called graces than virtues. These graces are ours only as they are consented to by our wills. They are not ours by choice and acquisition, but only by improvement and exercise. Though they agree with virtues in their matter and their end, yet they differ in their origin and form. For as all human actions flow from the will and the understanding, so do all virtues when they are rightly understood; whereas we are passive in the reception of the graces and they flow immediately from heaven.

15. And it is far more conducive to our happiness that we should conquer difficulties in the attainment of virtue than that we should be dead and idle while virtue is given to us in our sleep. We study, choose, desire, pursue, and labor after it, acquiring it finally by our own care and industry, with God's blessing upon it. For this cause God ordered our state and condition so that we should seek after it by our own labor, and so that we might be as well pleasing in his eyes and as honorable and admirable in the acquisition of

virtue as in the exercise and practice of it. And for these reasons God does not so often infuse it and is more desirous that we should by many repeated actions of our own attain it.

16. God does sometimes inspire it upon the general sloth of mankind, raising up some persons thereby to be like salt among corrupted men, lest all should putrefy and perish. Yet there is little reason why he should delight in that way, without some such unseemly and ungrateful necessity to compel him.

17. For any man to expect that God should break the general order and course of nature to make him virtuous without his own endeavors, is to tempt God by a presumptuous carelessness, and by a slothful abuse of his faculties to fulfill the parable of the unprofitable servant [Lk. 17:7–10].

18. The powers of the soul are not virtues themselves, but when they are clothed with virtuous operations they are transformed into virtues. For powers are in the soul just as limbs and members in the body, which may indifferently be applied to virtues and vices and can alike be busied and exercised in either.

19. As the members are capable of various motions, either becoming or deformed, and are one thing when they are naked and another when attired, and capable of being modified with the use of habits; so too are the powers and faculties of the soul. As they are in the nature of man without exercise, they are void and naked. But by many acts

of vice or virtue they put on a habit which seems chiefly to consist in an inclination and tendency to such actions. This tendency is a facility of working, an acquaintance with a form of action, a love to these powers of soul, and a delight in them. For by long custom, it turns to a second nature, and becomes at last as necessary as life itself; a confirmed habit being taken in and incorporated with the powers of the soul by frequent exercise.

20. (2) In the second definition we add that virtue is a right and well-ordered habit. A habit is something added to that which wears it. Every power of the soul is naked, without the quality by which long custom clothes it. Much of the formal reason of virtue is revealed in these words: right and well-ordered. For confused, irregular, and careless habits will always be erroneous and deformed. They must consequently end in dishonor and miseries. He must aim at the mark and hit it. Only those actions that are well guided produce right and well-ordered habits, which alone can carry us to our sovereign end.

21. A mind in good form is a soul clothed with right understandings: thoughts and affections well-ordered, principles and contrivances well proposed, means and ends rationally consulted, all considered, and the best chosen.[4]

---

[4] "A mind in good form" in the original was "a mind in frame," a term that Traherne seems to invent and which expresses a vision of the world we exist in as being in dynamic interplay with our minds. One need only think of the difference between the way human suffering looks to those who exist in the frame of Christian hope, versus to those who look at it from the frame of material science, to see that our frame provides us with much more than just context.

Long custom habituating us to the benefit and excellence of these things disposes the soul toward a right and well-ordered habit, or frame of spirit, which regards that glorious end for which we were created.

22. By force of this we attain our happiness. Idleness and virtue are as destructive to each other as fire and water. In all virtue there is some force, and in all force much action. A virtuous habit ceases to be virtuous unless it actually inclines us to virtuous operations. As the powers of the soul when they are well exerted turn into virtues, so it is by that exertion that we attain our happiness. Virtue is that right and well-ordered habit by force of which we attain our happiness.

23. Its force is never expressed but in exercise and operation. Yet even when we are asleep it may tacitly incline us and make us ready, when we awake, to be virtuous. Perhaps the habit sleeps and wakes with the body. But if the habit and its energy are the same thing, it still sleeps when its energy ceases. If they are different from one another then the habit may continue for some time without the force of its operation.

24. But it is not our purpose to divert into blind and obscure corners of inquiry, such as whether the soul of a man asleep may be made virtuous or not, or whether the habits continue in him while sleeping without their acts. It is sufficient that when he who has a virtuous habit is awake, he is in all his actions inclined and carried to his own happiness. Unless he falls into an oblivion worse than sleep,

some damnable and vicious lethargy, he is always mindful of his last end and tends towards it in a direct line.

25. All his actions derive a tincture from the first principle, that habit of soul by which he is carried toward his own happiness. All those actions that spring from that habit tend toward bliss, and by force of that habit are made virtuous, and are performed with facility.

26. All the difficulty is in the beginning. Virtues in the beginning are like green fruits, sour and imperfect, but their maturity is accompanied with sweetness and delight. It is hard to acquire a virtuous habit at first, but when it is once obtained it makes all virtue exceedingly easy, both happy and delightful. For a virtuous habit certainly acts according to its own nature, as the sun shines because it is constituted of light. It acts freely, yet when it does act it must act virtuously. It can do nothing else. For it is no virtuous habit but rather some other principle that exerts vicious and bad operations.

27. Happiness is with so much necessity the end of virtue that we cannot take a due estimate of the excellence of virtue without considering the tendency which it has to happiness. For as the unlimited means are absurd, and indeed false means that have no relation nor proportion to their end, so too would all the virtues be inept and worthless and no virtues at all if they did not in some sort bring about our happiness. For happiness is the adequate end that we seek by nature, whether it be in glory, or in pleasure, or in wealth or learning. All that is delightful and pleasing to our reason is comprehended in our happiness. If we desire to glorify

God, or to please the angels, or be grateful to men, it is because we love ourselves and delight in our own happiness. We have a good opinion of all those actions whereby we do so, either as a means or as a part of happiness, so that, when we are thinking about the diversity of virtues, however we divide them, and whatever makes them each glorious, we have to place them in their role as conduits to the last end of man: the end of man's blessedness and glory.

IV:

THE POWERS
AND AFFECTIONS OF THE SOUL

1. TWO THINGS are apparent to the eye in happiness: glory and treasure. The faculties of the soul affect both in multiple ways. The *understanding* was made to see the value of our treasure. The freedom of *will* was made to achieve glory by our actions. Likewise, *anger* was made to stir us up against all difficulty and opposition that might stand in our way. *Appetite* was made for us to pursue the pleasure in all states. *Fear* was made to heighten our concern, that we might more dread the danger of losing that happiness, in which no less than glory and treasure are infinitely united. *Reason* itself was made to allow us to compare felicities and weigh which is the most perfect. *Desire* was made to covet happiness; hope, to encourage us in the pursuit of it; *aversion*, for the avoiding of all temptations and impediments; *love*, for the goodness of it; *joy*, for its fruition; *hatred*, to keep us from the misery which is contrary to it; *boldness*, to attempt it; *sorrow* and *despair*, to punish and torment us if we fail to attain it. For sorrow and despair, being unpleasant affections, serve to engage us in the pursuit of happiness because we are loath to experience the sense of such troublesome passions.

2. *Ambition* and *covetousness* are inclinations of the soul. By the former we are carried to glory, by the latter to treasure. And, as with all the rest, so may these be made either virtues or vices: virtues when they are means conducive to the highest end and vices when they distract and entangle us with inferior objects.

3. The inclinations and affections of the soul may be defective or excessive in their exercise towards objects. In relation to the highest object there is no danger of excess. We can never too violently either love or desire our supreme happiness. Our hope can never exceed its greatness. We can never too much rejoice in the fruition of it, nor can we exceed in anger or hatred against those things that would bereave us of it. Nor can we fear too much the misery of that life which will be ever without it. We cannot be affected with too much sorrow and despair at the loss of it. But if we look upon inferior things, which are merely accidental to the nature of happiness, such as the favor of men, injuries, crosses, temporal successes, the beauty of the body, the goods of fortune, and such like, our affections and passions may be too excessive. This is because the good or evil of these is but finite, whereas the good of sovereign bliss is altogether infinite, and so is the evil of eternal misery.

4. When our own actions are well regulated, there is nothing in the world but what may be made conducive to our highest happiness. Nor is there any value in any object or creature in the world but that it is subservient to our bliss. No member of the body, no sense or endowment of any member, no inclination or faculty of the soul, no passion or affection, no virtue, no grace, no spiritual gift, no assistance,

no means of grace; nothing, no matter how great or precious, can be of any value except in order to achieve happiness. In truth, nothing without this can be great or estimable. Every virtue therefore must have this in common with all the laws and ordinances and works of God. All virtues must directly or obliquely tend to our supreme happiness—upon this depends all their excellency.

5. Some virtues are necessary in the estate of innocence, some in the estate of grace, and some in the estate of glory.

6. Without seeing, it is impossible to enjoy our happiness or find out the way to it. Therefore, knowledge is necessary in all estates; without loving knowledge, it is impossible to delight in its goodness. The work of righteousness is to render to every thing a due esteem. Without this it is apparent that no treasure, though in itself never so great, can be of any value to us. Holiness is the inner knowledge that we make of discharging our duty and the zeal with which we avoid the profaneness of its contrary. Goodness is necessary because without it we ourselves cannot be amiable, or be delightful to others, or enjoy ourselves, or acquire glory. The office of wisdom is to choose and pursue the highest end by the best of all means that can be chosen.

7. These are transcendent virtues, by which even God himself enjoys his happiness. They are incumbent on us by the law of nature. They are so essentially united to our formal happiness that no blessedness or glory can be enjoyed without them. Therefore, we are to look upon them as the life and soul of religion, as eternal duties in all states to be forever exercised. They are all exercised in the very

fruition itself. This will be seen more apparently when we come to each one of these virtues in particular. They were enjoined in the state of innocence, without any need of a positive law, by the very nature of God and the soul. They were directed by things themselves and must be exercised in the state of grace. And they will abide forever in the state of glory.

8. God gave us liberty so that virtues, which we bring about by work, might be ours. And that the results of these works would be virtues indeed, being brought about through difficult work. God desired that virtues might be ours and that we obtain them only with difficulty so that we might be much more laudable and glorious in our eternal condition. God gave us liberty, in the beginning, that we might choose what we would, and placed us in such an estate that, having in us only the seeds and principles of all virtue, we might exercise our natural powers of our own accord, to attain that actual knowledge, wisdom, and righteousness, wherein the perfection of our soul consists, and by which the perfection of our bliss is to be enjoyed. That, being naked by nature, though pure and clean, we might clothe ourselves with our own habits, attain the glory of those ornaments in our own acts, for which we were created, and work our own righteousness in such a way as God had appointed.

9. For the glory which we were to attain is that goodness which we are to show in our own voluntary care and obedience. That goodness is chiefly expressed in the kind and genuine exercise of our own liberty, while we are careful not to displease him to whom we are obliged. The purpose

of our freedom is that we are supposed to do the things that please God, even though we had no restraint upon us.

10. To make ourselves amiable and beautiful by the exercise of our own power produces another kind of beauty and glory than if we were compelled to be good by all his intervening power. All goodness is spoiled by compulsion. Our own actions, springing from an interior fountain deep within the soul, when voluntarily and freely exerted are more acceptable. And the will, whence they spring, is more excellent and perfect. This I would have you note well, for the intrinsic goodness and glory of the soul consists in the perfection of an excellent will. Without this it might be a piece of dirt surrounded with gold, but no imputed or annexed value could make it a jewel.

11. The actions of God, or of the angels, or of other men, towards the will add no value to the soul if it will do nothing of itself. If it is idle or inactive, the more excellent the actions of God and of all other creatures are towards it, the more deformed and perverse is the soul. Nor will all the glory of its powers and inclinations excuse it, but the more great and divine they are, the more abominable it will make itself by abusing them in frustrating their inclinations.

12. God removed all constraint and infused greater excellence and beauty into these holy actions which he required from man. For it pleased God to make men open to temptations, so that having obstacles to overcome and disadvantages to struggle with, man's righteousness might be more full of virtue, and man himself made capable of victory and triumph. For this end God seated man in a low

estate, even in an estate of trial. In this state was the occasion of exercising faith and hope, because his happiness was distant from him: faith in believing the promises of God, and hope in waiting for the accomplishment of his bliss. He had occasions for fear also, in relation to God's power and justice. God was able to remove his happiness upon the least offense, and to bring upon him that misery that was denounced for his transgression. In this estate of trial, prudence, which is conversant in low affairs, was to watch, consider, and direct man's behavior in the midst of those dangers and temptations that might possibly be expected. His temperance was to be exercised in the government of his appetite so that all inferior satisfactions and sensual pleasures might be limited and ordered as it most consists with his highest happiness. Humility was to be exercised in the acknowledgement of his own unworthiness, he who was taken out of nothing. And gratitude was to be exercised in a kind of just repayment to his benefactor, for all the glory to which he was given in advance.

13. All these virtues are in themselves delightful and easy in their exercise. They immediately elicit happiness and are by nature necessary to man's enjoyment of it. They are consonant to reason and agreeable to the circumstances of his happy condition. His fear and humiliation, which were the severest in paradise, were aided and comforted with a transcendent hope and assurance that upon his diligent care he might be eternally blessed.[1] He was aided also with the

---

[1] This is an odd bit of either theology or, at least, phraseology from Traherne. It is possible he is referring to the "fear and humiliation" which Adam and Eve experienced after the Fall, prior to their banishment from Eden. However, Traherne does

sweet sense of his happy change—a glorious admiration resulting from the comparison between his present estate and the estate to which he was to be exalted by his Creator.

14. I will not say that there were more virtues than these to be exercised in Eden. But by these, you may discern the nature of all virtues and infer that they must be qualities such as obedience to God and charity to one another.

15. All harsh and sour virtues came in by sin. We are to look upon them not as virtues intended by God and nature, but occasioned afterwards, because their use and existence is accidental.

16. When we fell into sin, we let death and misery into the world, contracted shame and guilt upon ourselves, defiled our nature with deformities and diseases, and on that occasion made many things necessary to our happiness that were not so before. Insofar as they have both a mixture of bitterness and advantage in them, we may thank ourselves for the bitterness and God for the advantage. For as by sin

---

not discuss virtue in fallen man until paragraph 15, and so may be referring to a fear and humiliation experienced in the state of innocence. To imagine "fear and humiliation" as being more severe in paradise than out of it must be related to a thinking that the greater fear was related to a greater wisdom, since the fear of the Lord is the beginning of wisdom (Prov. 9:10). "Fear" here is perhaps closer to our contemporary idea of "reverence." In the same way we would say that the virtuous know vice but the vicious are incapable of knowing virtue. Perhaps in this way our ancestors in paradise knew God more clearly, and so knew our current state as a possible future and trembled at it more than we do. Still, readers should note this is an idiosyncratic presentation by Traherne at best.

we forfeited our happiness, so a new obedience consisting in the practice of proper virtues was necessary to recover it. These virtues, whose names and natures were different in kind from those virtues which were natural to us in Eden, were virtues we had never heard of before, all which we must look upon, not as food, but as medicine, considering them under the notion of remedies—not focusing on how something in them is distasteful to sense even though, once we know the occasion for them, they are infinitely agreeable to reason.[2]

17. Virtues are but an equivocal offspring of the fall. Sin could never beget such beautiful children as meekness, repentance, patience, alms-deeds, self-denial, submission to the divine will, fortitude, contentment in all states, etc.

18. While there was no sin, there was no need of penitence. While there was no pain or misery, no need for patience. Without wrongs and injuries, there is no use of meekness. Where there is no poverty, there is no place for alms-deeds. There is no need for courage where there are no enemies. In Eden, there was no ignorance, nor any supernatural truths to be confirmed by miracles; therefore, apostles and

---

[2] Traherne's comparison here is between virtues in our fallen state and unpleasant medicines. Taking the latter means subjecting ourselves to unpleasant tastes and sensations—acts which, considered by themselves, are contrary to reason. However, when we focus instead on the health which the medicines bring, the act is perfectly reasonable. So too with postlapsarian virtues—in pursuing these we may subject ourselves to pain and difficulty, which seems unreasonable unless we have the end of the action in mind. Such a metaphor can be found as far back in philosophy as Plato's *Gorgias*.

prophets, ministers and doctors were superfluous there. So also tithes and temples, schools of learning, and masters and tutors were unnecessary. The unsavory duty incumbent on parents to chastise their children was not requisite. For as all would have been instructed by the light of nature, so would all have been innocent and just and upright. No magistrate would have been needful to put any to shame, no courts of judicature, nor lawyers in the world. No buying and selling and therefore no commutative justice. The blessed earth had naturally been fertile and abounded with rich and glorious provisions. Nakedness had been the splendor and ornament of men, as it will be in heaven. The glorious universe had been their common house and temple, their bodies fitted for all seasons. There was no alien or stranger, no want, distress, or war. Rather there was all peace, plenty, and prosperity. It was all pleasure, and all were fellow citizens of the world. Masters and servants had been unknown. Had we continued in that estate, all would have enjoyed the liberty of kings. There would have been no dominion except that of husbands and fathers, a sweet and gentle dominion and a free relation. I can see no use that there had been of trades and occupations, only the pleasant diversion that Adam had in tending to the garden. I am sure that there had been no funerals, no sickness, no medicine nor any physicians. There had been no faith in the incarnation of the Son of God, because there was no occasion for that incarnation. There had been no ceremonial law of Moses, no baptism, nor the Lord's Supper because there were no supernatural mysteries to be typified. Rather there was the clear light of a divine reason and a free communion with God in the right discharge of those virtues, both divine and moral, which naturally belong to the estate of innocence. It would be right for those original and primitive virtues to continue. As it stands, sin and corruption has put a mask or visor of ordinances and new duties upon the face of religion. Though we have forgotten the virtues of our first estate and are apt now to terrify ourselves with that disguise by which we have concealed their beauty, by regarding only the virtues that were occasioned by sin and misery as real.

19. It is a great error to mistake the visor for the face or to see only the outward appearance of things. We commit this great error when we mistake the alterations and additions that are made after the fall of man for the whole business of religion. And yet this new constellation of virtues that appears after the Fall is almost the only thing talked of and understood in the world. The other duties, which are the soul of piety, are unknown. The reason for these, together with their origin and occasion, remains unseen. On account of this, religion appears like a sour and ungrateful thing to the world, impertinent to bliss, and void of reason. God is suspected and hated, and atheism enters the world and is there entertained.

20. To conceive of God as wise and good is an idea congenial to the notion of God. If we cannot see some reason in his ways, we are likely to suspect there is no deity; or, if there is, that he is malevolent and tyrannical, which is worse than none, for all wisdom and goodness are contained in love. If it is true that God is love, he will show it in our beings by making us great and excellent creatures. He will show this love in his gifts and bounties, by surrounding us with real and serviceable treasures. This love

will also be seen in all his laws, as well as in all his works, both of which are concerned about our welfare. And as he makes the world glorious and beautiful for us to dwell in, so will he make all necessary actions and virtues excellent and divine. He will impose no duties but such as those which are full of reason and lead us to bliss and glory more advantageously.

21. We are apt to charge our own faults to God, confusing all things. We do this because we do not see how penitence, meekness, and acts of charity, in relieving the poor, directly and immediately bring us into bliss. We are apt to fret at their imposition. But when we see all these virtues in their objects and their uses, the ends for which and the occasions on which they were introduced, we see that all are delightful to the reason of man's soul. They show how God is adored and admired for the depth of his wisdom and goodness, and beloved for the equity and excellency of his proceedings. For all these occasional virtues are but temporary; when our life, and this present world, are past and gone as a dream, love, joy, and gratitude will be all that will continue forever. In that future state, wisdom and knowledge, goodness and righteousness, and true holiness shall abide. The souls of all that are blessed will be transformed in life and glory. Repentance shall be gone and patience will cease. Faith and hope will be realized, right reason will be extended to all objects in all worlds, and eternity in all its beauties and treasures will be seen, desired, esteemed, and enjoyed.

22. Let it be your care to dive to the bottom of true religion and not suffer your eyes to be dazzled by its superficial appearance. Rest not in the help and remedies that it brings,

but search for the hidden manna and the substantial food underneath. Only this is the satisfaction of all wishes and desires, the true and celestial pleasures, and the causes of love and praise. True religion is thanksgiving founded in the manifestations of God's eternal favor, especially in the ends, for the sake of which all help and remedies are prepared.[3] For it is exceeding true that his laws are sweeter than the honey and the honeycomb; they are far more precious than thousands of pieces of gold and silver [Ps. 19:10].

---

[3] "Ends" here in the sense of *telos*.

V:
KNOWLEDGE DEFINED

1. KNOWLEDGE and love are so necessary to happiness that there can be no enjoyment or delight without them. Heaven and earth would be dark and obscure, angels and men would be vain and unprofitable, all creatures would be base and unserviceable, and happiness would be impossible were there no knowledge. Even God himself, without knowledge and love, could not very well exist, for his very essence is seated in infinite knowledge.

2. God is light, and in him is no darkness at all [1 Jn. 1:5]; he is love by nature and there is no hatred in his essence [1 Jn. 4:8]. His very Godhead is all perfection, by the infinite knowledge and love in his nature.

3. The origin of our knowledge is his Godhead: his essence and his will are the fountain of it. And the stream is so excellent that in all estates it is forever to be continued, as the light and glory of the whole creation.

4. The understanding power, which is seated in the soul, is the matter of that act in which the essence of knowledge consists. Its form is the act itself, whereby that power of knowing apprehends its object. Its nature is invisible, like that of all other spirits, simple and uncompounded. Its form

and matter are the same, for all powers, when transformed into act, are acts themselves. And the faculty of understanding, in a complete and perfect act of knowledge, attains its perfection and exerts its power in its exercise. Every act is power exerted.

5. The power of knowing is vain if not reduced into act. The soul is a melancholy and dreadful cave, a dungeon of darkness if void of knowledge. Had God himself a power of knowing distinct from its operation, and if he never exercised that power, it would be useless to him. His glory and blessedness are seated in the light of that knowledge, which to us upon earth appears inaccessible.

6. If we would be perfect, as our Father who is in heaven is perfect [Mt. 5:48], our power of knowing must be transformed into act. All objects must appear in the interior light of our own understanding. For even if all eternity were full of treasures, and the whole world with all the creatures in it transformed into joys, if we were ignorant of them we would continue as poor and empty as if there were nothing but vacuity and space. For not to be, and not to appear, are the same thing to the understanding.

7. Were a man a seraph by his essence, or something by nature more glorious and divine than the highest order of the most blessed angels, or yet the greatest creature that almighty power was able to produce, his soul and body would signify nothing if he were unknown to himself and unaware of his excellence.

8. If you would have a solid prospect of any virtue, you must understand that virtues are powers transformed into right, wise, and regular acts. They avoid all extremes of negligence on the one hand and excess on the other. The extremes of knowledge are ignorance and error.

9. For you ought to know that heaven and earth are as full of treasures as almighty power was able to create them. You, by nature, are the best and highest of all possible creatures, made like God for the highest and best of all possible ends. And you are called to live in communion with him in all his fruitions. But, being vilely corrupted, you have lost the sense of all these realities and are ignorant of the excellences of your own state and nature.

10. I know for certain that God is infinite in wisdom, goodness, and power. Nothing is wanting on his part to perfect your desires. But *you* may be blind, idle, ignorant, and dead in a certain manner. Although you want to perfect yourself, and have need of nothing but clear and perfect apprehensions, your apprehensions are sottish and erroneous at present, they may make you miserable, and poor, and blind, and naked.[1]

---

[1] "Sottish" is an archaic but evocative word which we felt compelled to leave in its original form. It is an adjectival form which indicates that some person is in the state of being a "sot" or, to use synonyms, a blockhead, a dolt, a *fool*. It is one of those earthy gems which come down to us from the Old English (spelled with two t's and sometimes with an e: "sott" or "sotte") and since it has made it thus far we have an obligation to preserve it and pass it on to posterity. Beginning in the sixteenth century, it began seeing wider usage and took on the added characteristic of implying someone was a drunk.

11. If sin had been like Circe's cup, changing the shape of man's body to that of a swine or dragon, the depravation of his nature would have been plain and visible. Yet without knowing what kind of form he had before, it would not appear so visible, because we would be insensible of his first form and unable to compare the one with the other. But sin is a moral *slanting*, and the change it produces in the soul is spiritual.[2] It makes a man to differ far more from himself than any alteration of body can do. But sin so blinds man's understanding that he does not remember what he was in his first parent. The first man (who had experience of both states) was able to compare them because, in his corruption, he retained a sense of that nature and life which he enjoyed in his integrity. Yet all his posterity, born sinners, never were sensible of the light and glory of an innocent estate. On account of this, they may be wholly ignorant both of God and of themselves, utterly unable to conceive the glory of the world or of that relation wherein they should by nature have stood towards all the creatures.

12. It is impossible to conceive how great a change a slight action may produce. But press the wick a little with one's finger, and a lamp is extinguished; darkness immediately overspreads the room. The glory and splendor of the whole world would vanish upon the extinction of the sun; one instant of cessation from the emission of its beams would be its extinction. A soul is a more glorious thing than the

---

[2] "Slanting" here is my rendering of Traherne's "obliquity," almost certainly used in place of the Latin *obliquitas*. The connotation is twofold: one sense is that of geometry, of the angle which deviates from the horizontal or vertical; the other is in the sense of perversity. *Incurvatus in se* comes to mind as a near parallel.

sun: the sphere of its activity is far greater and its light more precious. All the world may be filled with the splendor of its beams; eternity itself was prepared for it! Were there but one soul to see and enjoy all the creatures, upon the suspension of its light, all the creation would be rendered vain. Light itself is but darkness without the understanding.

13. The existence of many souls is so far from decreasing the value of one that it is by reason of their multitude more useful and excellent. For the value of the objects imputes a luster and higher value to the light in which they are enjoyed. So, if souls themselves are more excellent than all other creatures, then they should be enjoyed alongside and in fact above all other aspects of creation. And the power of the soul which allows for the enjoyment of them is more to be esteemed and should be acknowledged as such. This most divine part of the most divine part is the understanding. And the thing the soul chiefly enjoys is the knowledge of God himself and his holy angels. Those felicities and glories, which the sun cannot extend to, the soul can comprehend. All of these, since their fruition depends upon that act of the understanding by which they are considered, reflect a luster. They add a value to that knowledge by which the soul attains them. It follows that the infinite value of all these is seated in the intellect. And as the power, so the act of knowledge on which their fruition depends, is of infinite use and excellency. As the loss is infinite when the soul is bereaved of them, so is the damage. It suffers by the failing of its light, whether that defect be voluntary or imposed by some outward impediment.

14. As for the use of knowledge, it is apparent enough. The relation between the use and excellency of things is near and intimate; nothing useless can be at all excellent and every excellence in every being is founded in its usefulness. The use of souls is as great as their excellency; the use of knowledge is as endless in variety as in extent and value.

15. Knowledge is that which illuminates the soul, enkindles love, excites our care, inspires the mind with joy, informs the will, enlarges the heart, and regulates the passions. It unites all the powers of the soul to their objects, sees their beauty, understands their goodness, discerns our interest in them, forms our apprehensions of them, and considers and enjoys their excellences. All contentments, raptures, and ecstasies are conceived in the soul. They are begotten by knowledge; all laws, obligations, and rewards are understood by knowledge. All virtues and graces of the mind are framed by knowledge, all advantages are by it improved, all temptations discerned, all dangers avoided, all affairs ordered, and all endowments acquired. All the ornaments of life, all the beauties of the inward man, and all the works of piety are affected by knowledge. In the light of knowledge all pleasures arise, and as fruits and flowers are begotten in the earth by the beams of the sun, so do all kinds of joy spring from the creatures and are made ours by the help of that knowledge that shines on them. Its last offspring are eternal thanksgivings and praises. The divine image and the perfection of bliss are sounded in knowledge. God himself dwells in the soul, with all his attributes and perfections, by knowledge. By knowledge we are made temples of the Holy Ghost, and partakers of the divine nature. For this cause it is that St. Paul prays that we might

be filled with the knowledge of his will in all wisdom and spiritual understanding, that we might walk worthy of the Lord unto all pleasing, being fruitful in every good work, and increasing in the knowledge of God, strengthened with all might according to his glorious power, unto all patience and long-suffering, with joyfulness giving thanks to the Father. That Father who has made us fit to be partakers of the inheritance of the saints in light, who has delivered us from the power of darkness, and translated us into the kingdom of his dear Son [Col. 1:9–12].

16. The sun is a glorious creature and its beams extend to the utmost stars. By shining on them, it clothes them with light and by its rays excites all their influences. It enlightens the eyes of all the creatures; it shines on forty kingdoms at the same time, on seas and continents in a general manner. Yet so particularly does it regard all that every speck in the air, every grain of dust, every sand, and every spire of grass is wholly illuminated by it, as if the sun did entirely shine upon that alone. Nor does it only illuminate all these objects in an idle manner. Rather, its beams are operative, entering in and filling the pores of things with spirits.[3] It impregnates

---

[3] "Spirits" in the sense of "spiritedness," rather than to do with angels or fairies or some such. This usage is likely in the same sense as discussed by C. S. Lewis in "Appendix A" of his *Miracles*, being drawn from the now obsolete pre-modern belief in "extremely fine fluids in the human body called 'the spirits,'" to which Lewis attributes the origins of phrases such as "in high spirits." C. S. Lewis, *Miracles* (London: William Collins, 2012), 278. A fuller explanation of the ancient idea in Galen and Aristotle can be found in James J. Bono, "Medical Spirits and the Medieval Language of Life," *Traditio* 40 (1984): 91–130. The examples of growth and expending energies in the following sentences should be instructive.

them with powers, causing all their emanations, odors, virtues, and operations. Springs, rivers, minerals, and vegetables are all perfected by the sun; all motion, life, and sense of birds, beasts, and fish depend on the same. Yet the sun is but a little spark among all the creatures that are made for the soul; the soul, being the most high and noble of all, is capable of far higher perfections, far more full of life and vigor in its uses. The sphere of its activity is unlimited, its energy is endless upon all its objects. It can exceed the heavens in its operations and run out into infinite spaces. Such is the extent of knowledge; it seems to be the light of all eternity. All objects are equally near to the splendor of its beams: as innumerable millions may be conceived in its light, with a ready capacity for millions more. So too can it penetrate all abysses and reach to the center of all nature. It can converse with all beings: visible and invisible, corporeal and spiritual, temporal and eternal, created and uncreated, finite and infinite, substantial and accidental, actual and possible, imaginary and real. All the mysteries of bliss and misery and all the secrets of heaven and hell are objects of the soul's capacity here. They will be seen and known from this time forward.

17. Were almighty power magnified by filling eternity with created objects and were all the omnipresence of God full of joys, it is able, when assisted by his divine knowledge, to look upon all. And though every one of them should have an infinite depth within, an endless variety of uses, a relation to all the rest of the world, the soul, as if it were able to contract all its strengths, from all the expansions of eternity and space, and fix them upon this moment, or on this center, entirely beholding this alone, in all its fullness, can

see its original, its end, its operations, effects, and properties, as if it had nothing to consider but this alone, in a most exquisite and perfect manner.

18. It cannot be denied that every being in all worlds is an object of the understanding. Nor can the Psalmist be doubted: "in his presence there is fullness of joy, and at his right hand there are pleasures forevermore" [Ps. 16:11]. That is, his omnipresence is full of joys and his eternity of riches and pleasures. It cannot be denied that the soul is by its creation intended for the throne of God. For the soul is made capable of his omnipresence and eternity, and, as the Apostle speaks, may be filled with all the fullness of God [Eph. 3:19]. This is commensurate with the immensity of his eternal power, which you will see more when we address the virtues of love, wisdom, righteousness, and holiness. Here, we need only note that nature never made any power in vain, but ever intends the perfection of what it produces. Nature prepares objects for the understanding; the perfection of this power is the actual attainment of the knowledge of which it is capable.

19. The principal objects of our knowledge are God and man's self. Relative to God, the objects of our knowledge are the kingdom of God, his laws and works, his ways in all ages, and his counsels and his attributes. For man's self, the objects of our knowledge are man's interest and duty, the transactions of the world, and the thoughts and actions of angels and men. Though these may be less material objects of the understanding, in relation to God and a man's self, they are of great importance.

20. God, as he is the life and fountain of all happiness, is most fit to be known. He is the end of all perfection, the Creator of our being, almighty in power, infinite in wisdom and goodness, author of the universe, and Lord of all the creatures. Plato makes him the very light of the understanding. He affirms that as three things are necessary to vision—the eye rightly prepared, the object suitably seated, and light to convey the idea to the eye—so there are three things required to complete and perfect intelligence: an understanding eye, an intelligible object, and a light intelligible in which to conceive it.[4] This last is God. The royal Psalmist and divine philosopher David is not far from the notion when he says, "In thy light we shall see light" [Ps. 36:9]. For God is the light of the understanding. His nature is the light of all the creation. Therefore, it is said by Christ himself that the knowledge of God is life eternal [Jn. 17:3]. For his light is the life of men, and without him we can do nothing [Jn. 1:4]. Until we know his nature, we cannot apprehend the excellency of his works, for all their goodness is derived from him and ends in him. His love moved him to create the world, and the principal end for which it was made is the glory of the Creator in the happiness of his creatures. The glory of the creatures is seen in his glory. By his wisdom and goodness we are guided to the hope and investigation of their excellence. His infinite bounty made them all our treasures, that for the perfection of their beauty and worth we might celebrate his praises.

21. He that would not be a stranger to the universe, an alien to happiness, and a foreigner to himself must know God to

---

[4] Possibly Plato, *Republic*, 507b–509c.

be an infinite benefactor. All eternity is full of treasures, the world itself is the beginning of gifts, and his own soul is the possessor of all, in communion with the deity. The business of religion is contentment in God, who never laid aside his wisdom in any operation of his power and never forgot to make the least of his works agreeable to his goodness. Rather, he is so perfect that his infinite goodness, wisdom, and power are wholly exerted and made wholly conspicuous in every operation. It is the beauty of truth that makes knowledge of such infinite value. For if we know that all the treasures of wisdom and knowing be ordained for a wise and knowing man; if all objects in the clear light of heaven and eternity be laudable and glorious; if divine wisdom has so far grasped that the number and value of God's gifts is accurate and exactly answerable to the nature of its causes; if every soul that will live in his image may be the friend of God and acquire the empire of the world and be beloved of angels and admired of men; and if fruition is the end of knowledge and all things made that they may be enjoyed, then we can say knowledge is the only thing that enriches the soul, and the knowing man is the friend of God. The exercise and pleasure of this divine friendship is the end of the creation and the perfection of the soul.

22. The knowledge of a man's self is highly conducive to his happiness, not only as it gives him power to rejoice in his excellency, but as it shows him the end for which he was created. For by knowing what inclinations and powers are in his soul, he discerns what is agreeable with and fit for his essence. He perceives what objects and what operations are conducive to his welfare and what means he is to use for the attainment of his end. He also finds what that end consists

of, where his perfection is found. If the powers of his soul are unlimited, his desire infinite, and his reach eternal; if he is able to see and enjoy all worlds and all that is above all worlds in the image of God; if his ambition drives him to be pleasing to all angels and men and to be glorious in the eyes of all kingdoms and ages; and if his abilities are exhaustless for the fruition of all that is excellent in eternity itself, it is a token that he is ordained for God and the enjoyment of his kingdom. It would be a wicked folly to restrain himself to the miserable contentment of a cell or cottage and to delight in nothing but some fragments of the creation; these, in comparison to the whole, are infinitely defective.

23. Of all other things I would have this most deeply engraved in the mind: that God has exceeded all imagination in the works of his hands; that he who overcomes shall be the son of God and inherit all things; that there is an infinite end when the secrets of all hearts shall at last be revealed; that in heaven all thoughts and things shall be known; that the kingdom of heaven is infinitely glorious; that all the blessed are perfect sovereigns, every one the possessor and end of it all; that all things proceeding immediately from God are the best that are possible; that the best and the worst things, as ordered by him, are perfectly amiable and subservient to happiness; that he himself alone has a proper right to all that is excellent; that God is in every thing to be enjoyed; that he is enjoyed only when his essence and his works satisfy the desires of perfect reason and exceed all wishes in filling and delighting the soul; that having filled the soul with infinite wisdom, he has laid infinite obligations upon us, and set infinite rewards before us; that he has made

laws infinitely amiable and given us duties infinitely desirable; for all these things he deserves eternal adorations and thanksgivings.

VI:
LOVE AND HATRED

1. BECAUSE love is the most desirable employment of the soul, the power of loving is to be accounted the most high and noble of the faculties. Love is not seated by itself in the mind, but attended with a mighty outgoingness and inclination.

2. There is no creature so unsociable and furious that it is incapable of loving something or other. Wolves and tigers live at peace among themselves. Lions have a fondness for their grim mistresses. Even the ugliest bear has a natural affection for its whelps, which is expressed in rage when they are bereaved of them. Things void of love must be either absolutely dead or live in misery. Whatsoever is endowed with life and sense delights in simple and grateful operations. Love is a necessary affection of their souls. It is impossible to grasp anything delightful unless it is pleasing, and whatever is pleasing must be lovely. For to be pleased and to love are the same thing. If there is any difference between the two, the pleasure we take in any object is the root of that desire which we call love. Affection, by which we pursue the pleasure that is grasped in it, is part of the love that we bear unto it. The end of this is the completion of that pleasure which it first perceives: all is love variously

modified, according to the circumstances in which the object is represented.

3. As love is the only easy and delightful operation, so hatred of all others is the most troublesome and tormenting. Displeasure and enmity are the ingredients of its nature; its fruits are as bitter as gall and wormwood. Murder, vexation, and grief along with separation, contention, and horror are the offspring of the one; peace and embraces, praises and complacencies, honors, services, benefits, and pleasures are the fruit of the other. These are the little cupids that fly about this celestial Venus, when she is what she ought to be: the mother of happiness and the daughter of God.

4. All creatures that are sensible of pain or pleasure must of necessity be addicted to love and hatred; that is, to the love of what is pleasing and to the hatred of what is painful. And if any ask, which of these twins is the firstborn? The answer is that they may seem twins in respect of time, but in respect to nature love is the firstborn and the mother of hatred. For where nothing to be hated appears, pleasant things are beloved for their own sake. But if there were no pleasant thing to be beloved, nothing could be hated. Nothing could be hurtful because where there is no love, there is no interest, and where there is no concern, there can be no affection, no fear, or hope, or joy, or sorrow.

5. As fire begets water by melting ice, so does love beget contrary passions in the soul of a living creature: anger, malice, envy, grief, and jealousy. It does not do this by its own nature, but by the accidental interposition of some obstacle that hinders or endangers the fruition of its object.

Were there no love of ease and pleasure, there could be no anger or quarrel between competitors. Were there no emulation or desire, there could be no aversion or endeavor. All enmity and hostility springs either from contention, who shall enjoy what is desirable, or from some other principle of envy or revenge in relation to what is good. This is obvious in daily experience.

6. Life and love are so individually united that to live without loving something is impossible. Even in hell, where their whole life seems to be spent in detestation and hatred, actual love, like a fire under those embers, is covered and continued. If they could put off self-love, the love of happiness and interest, their torments would be gone. Punishments and rewards are impossible things where there is not self-love; for without something to love, pains and joys are equally agreeable.

7. As love is the root of endeavor, so it is the spring of all the passions; they all depend upon love alone. We are angry at that which stands in our way, between our love and its object. We desire an absent good because we love it. We hope for it when we consider its attainment feasible. We rejoice in it when we have it, and we fear to lose it. We grieve when it is gone, we despair if we cannot get or recover it, and we hate all that is opposite to it. Our love, when well regulated, is the greatest virtue. Upon the right choice of its object, and true government of itself, all the powers and affections of the soul are well employed. When we love all that we ought as we ought to, we fulfill all laws. When we hope and fear, hate and grieve, desire and rejoice on account of love, we do everything in a regular manner.

8. There is a sensual and brutish love and a human and divine love. Brutish love is of two sorts: the one springs from a harmony of complexions and a sympathy of bodies, while the other springs from the abstracted consideration of pleasure. The first of these is occasioned by a secret and inexpressible agreement of tempers, by which upon the presence of each other the senses are delighted. We know not why, this pleasure being a mystery in nature. It is perhaps founded in a grateful transpiration of spirits from one to the other.

9. The consideration of beauty seems peculiar to the love of men. No beast is observed to make any distinction between lineaments and features, nor upon any account of shape and colors to be delighted with each other. However, man exceeds the capacity of beasts in being able to note and admire the workmanship of God in the decent order of symmetry and proportion.

10. Human affection and divine love are nearly allied, yet are of several kinds. If you take the love of reason in its utmost height, it is always divine. It is conformable to the love of God both in its measures and degrees and in its effects and causes. The love of God is itself the love of perfect reason. As the reason of his love is infinite and eternal, so is its operation. But in a lower manner, human love differs from divine. Human love is founded upon temporal causes: vivacity, wit, learning, beauty, behavior, moral honesty, fidelity, kindness, goodness, power, majesty, wealth, nobility, worth, virtue, and the like. But all these may be exalted when they are sanctified. They may be made divine by the superadded concurrence of celestial causes. For when

a man loves another, because he is made in the image of God and by the beauty of his soul is something more than human, this love is made sacred and receives a grace from the influences of religion.

11. Divine love, strictly speaking, is founded on eternal causes. It is agreeable to the life of heaven, delightful to God, and pleasing to the angels. If divine love is taken in the highest sense, it is only in God. For it is his peculiar prerogative to love without obligation or reward, to be the sole author of all happiness, and to overflow with goodness of himself freely, without any motive, to go before the beauty and existence of his object, and to love from all eternity in an immutable manner. This is the nature of divine love. Even here there are infinite ends and causes of his love, though they are all in himself. For he loves that he may love, and begets that love which is his essence. His love is the foundation of all his treasures, the cause and end of the whole creation. It is this love alone by which he proceeds from himself to all his creatures, and by those to himself again for ever. All his kingdom, greatness, and pleasure, all his wisdom and goodness, all his life and perfection are seated in love. This love is his beauty and his holiness, his bounty and his Godhead. He loves in order that he may be all beauty, goodness, and holiness and that he may enjoy himself and the eternal pleasure of his essence in glory and blessedness forever.

12. It is God alone that loves by his essence; angels and men may love by inclination, but their affection is accidental to their nature, begins in time, and may alter or cease. It is subject to chance, obligation, and reward. It ought to be

guided according to the pleasure of a higher agent. In this it differs from the love of God, but in many things there is a great agreement and proportion between them. For God has made the love of angels and men so like his own, by extending their knowledge to all objects, that infinite perfections are contained in their love. This love is as godlike as anything created is capable of being; for almighty power and infinite wisdom are employed in the production of it.

13. For the better understanding of this love, we will consider it in three ways: in the power of loving, in the inclination to love, and in its act and perfection. It may seem a surprising truth, but the power of loving is as necessary to blessedness and glory as life itself. The inclination to love is as necessary as the power, and the act of love as necessary as the inclination. The world is useless without life, and life without love, the body without the soul, the soul without the power of loving, the power of loving without the inclination, and the inclination without the act.

14. In the power of loving, I shall note nothing at present except its extent and capacity. In beasts it is confined, but in men it is endless. As a beast is unable to examine what spaces are above the heavens, so is it unable to extend its affections beyond the memory of things perceived. A beast cannot represent to itself the ideas of its parents, nor can it see into ages that are before its birth or contemplate objects that will be after it is dead. But man can see, know, and love any object in any age or kingdom in the world. He can look into any region, though it is far removed, and converse easily with any person there. Once the place or the person is

presented to him in a clear light, he can communicate with them as he can with any object in his own country. He can look into Eden and consider Adam's dust in its first creation and survey the procedure of God in the works of his six days of creation. He can then pass out of time into eternity itself and run up to the origin and fountain head of all existence. He can here ponder the nature of God, search in his bosom for his eternal counsels, pierce into the center of the earth, and survey the circumference of all immensity. His love can follow his knowledge in all its flights; in spirit he can be present with all the angels. He is able to love not only his family and relations, but all the city and country where he lives. He can love all the cities and kingdoms in the world, all the generations in all kingdoms, all the spirits of just men made perfect, all the cherubim and seraphim, and our forever blessed God. The capacity of love is so all sufficient that his affection is not diminished but increased; the more he loves one, the more he is able, and the more he is inclined to love all that are united to him. As in ordinary friendship, the more we love the father, the more we love his wife and all his children. For the more we love any person, the more we love all that love him or are beloved by him. As the reasons of our love increase, so may our love itself; the capacity of love being so inexhaustible that it can never be exceeded or surmounted by its object.

15. The capacity of love being so exceedingly vast, it multiplies and heightens in the soul of man such that it is apt to overflow of its own accord. For nothing is so prone to communicate itself as that active principle of love. The soul which is generous and divine is disposed to the exercise of love; therein it finds its proper element. The very sun is

not more inclined to communicate its beams than the soul is inclined to love. For the soul, being made in the image of God who is love by his essence, must be like him in power and inclination. The soul is made for nothing else but the attainment of its perfection, so that it can never rest until it actually loves in the manner of God's likeness. It must, of necessity, have an operation. For as all life is founded in action, so also is all pleasure.

16. If love is considered in all its perfection, all that is lovely is beloved by the soul. All the capacity of love is filled with its objects, and all the goodness of the Creator and his creatures is at once enjoyed. Love is the life and pleasure and enlargement of the soul; it is the wisdom, goodness, and glory of the soul. I confess that there are many errors and diseases in love. A vicious love is always miserable in its effects. Yet it so bewitches the senses that the soul, being captivated by the force of present delight, is violently carried in an irresistible appetite to those things which reason condemns and advises to shun as evil. Medea's faction most prevails in the world: *Video meliora proboque, deteriora sequor.* [1]

---

[1] Medea is most famous as the mythic wife of Jason the Argonaut. She appears in Hesiod's *Theogony* and most famously as the titular character of Euripides's *Medea.* Her story varies in the telling, so the specific meaning implied by Traherne is not known here. However, he does use the phrase in another place, his *Early Notebooks* from his days at Oxford (one of which has survived to us and can be found under "Manuscripts of Thomas Traherne" at the Bodleian Library, Oxford). On page 153 of this notebook, in a section discussing his recent reading of Bacon, he writes, "It's a common Maxim, *Voluntas sequitur ultimum Dictamen Intellectus* [the will follows the final dictate of the intellect]; but fouly falsified by those of Medea's faction; *video eliora proboque, deteriora sequor* [I see better things but approve of and follow worse ones]." Bacon

17. Love is a vice when irrational and illegal, rebellious and sensual, blind and defective, unjust and absurd. It is a vice when evil things are beloved, when good things are preferred above the better, and when the best things are neglected.

18. Virtuous love is that which proceeds from a well governed understanding. It is seated in a will that is guided by reason. Virtuous love renders to all things their just due and is the powerful parent of all kinds of virtues. This love may be considered either in its properties or effects. The latter relates to the soul itself and to the conversation of the whole man. When it is well understood, it will be found the proper and immediate means by which we attain our perfection and happiness.

---

himself does not mention Medea in the section of the book which Traherne indicates he was annotating, but does, curiously, several chapters later. Without speculating too much on the meaning of "Medea's faction" or the repetition of it in his writings we can fairly say that it represents the bodily or appetitive part in opposition to the mind or the rational part. For more on this, see: Carol L. Marks, "Thomas Traherne's Early Studies," *The Papers of the Bibliographical Society of America* 62, no. 4 (1968): 511–36.

VII:
HOW GOD BENEFITS FROM LOVE

1. BEFORE we can fully discern the benefit of love, or see the glory of it in all its high and admirable effects, we must consider what love is and does in God. As we have said, the life of God is love. The Apostle John says that God is love and by loving he begot his love. If his love be his Godhead, his essence is an infinite and eternal act of love. Through this love, which extends across all infinity and loves eternally, he begot his infinite and eternal essence.[1] This is the love that fills all worlds with beauty and glory. When you consider it well, it is clear that an act of love is begotten by loving. His wisdom, goodness, blessedness, and glory are seated in love. Because of this, his love is his wisdom. This wisdom is the Son of God: his goodness, his glory, and his

---

[1] Taken to mean "God from God," or consubstantiality, this is a fine if idiosyncratic phrase. Bear in mind Traherne is writing a work of ethics for a non-academic audience, not engaging directly in Trinitarian theology. Still, we want to make clear that one should not read this as saying that the essence of God is distinct from his existence such that the essence was begotten by a preexisting deity. That would be profoundly heretical. Rather, to circle back to my starting point, read this as saying "the Father begat one of identical essence." For more see the chapters on the doctrine of God in the *Synopsis of a Purer Theology*, ed. William den Boer and Riemer A. Faber (Landrum, SC: Davenant Press, 2023).

blessedness. All these, though we conceive of them diversely, are the same thing. It is said that the Son of God is the wisdom of the Father and the brightness of his Father's glory [1 Cor. 1:24; Heb. 1:3]. He is the life of the Father, by whom he made the worlds. He is the love of the Father, for whom all things were created that are in heaven and that are in earth, visible and invisible, whether they be thrones, or dominions, or principalities, or powers; all things were created by him, and for him [Col. 1:16]. For God enjoys all things by his love, which is his eternal Son. He made them as perfect and delightful as it was possible for created things to be, in order that he might take pleasure in them. As he himself is made glorious and delightful in the eyes of all angels and men by love, so does his whole kingdom arise and spring from love. The beauty and happiness of all his creatures, their joys and praises as well as their uses and perfections, are founded in his love. By his love he begets all his pleasures in himself; by his love he made his treasures infinite. By this love alone does he take infinite pleasure and delight in himself and his kingdom. This is what the love of God accomplishes.

2. Had God not loved from all eternity, had he never desired nor delighted in anything, then he would never have exerted his almighty power, never communicated his goodness, nor begot his wisdom, never enjoyed himself, never applied himself to the production of his works, nor ever appeared in his glory to any eye whatsoever. Removing his love, we remove all the properties and effects of his essence and are utterly unable to conceive any idea of his Godhead. For if his power, though it is almighty, were dead and idle it would be fruitless and deformed. Idle power is not the essence of

the deity but a mere privation and vacuity. It would be at most a positive being as ignoble as it is inactive. The reason for his works is founded in love. So are all the obligations that are laid upon his creatures to adore him. All their rewards are founded in love and prepared by love: all his laws are the laws of love, all his attributes and counsels are love. These are in several forms, acting upon several occasions. When his love communicates itself in joy to innocent creatures, it is goodness. When it attains the most perfect end by the most perfect means, it is wisdom. When it rescues guilty creatures from hell, it is mercy. When it punishes the rebellious, it is justice. When it inspires obedience into any obstinate person, it is grace. When it delights in the beauty of all its works, it is blessedness. When it appears in the perfection of its works, it is glory. For glory is the perfection of beauty that arises from, and is seated in, the luster of excellent actions. It discovers the internal properties of an excellent agent, which is by those properties and actions made delightful to all judicious spectators.

3. Nor is it only in God, but also in us that the fruits and benefits of love are ineffable. For by loving as it ought to, the soul acquires its own perfection and is united to all its objects. By loving as it ought, it is made holy, wise, good, and amiable. Only by loving does it embrace the delights of which it is capable. Love is the root and soul of those actions for which a creature is desired and praised by others.

4. It is an infinite advantage that we are able to live in God's image, if we please. For if God alone is infinitely glorious and blessed, there is no way for us to become glorious and

blessed except by being made, by ourselves or by some other, like him.

5. By nature he has implanted the likeness of his power. This we are to improve by grace, turning it into act after his likeness. To be able to love is neither grace nor virtue, but a mere gift of God. It is a natural endowment which may be destroyed or completed. To actually love is the work of virtue, for by that act we enjoy our happiness.

6. Had God limited and confined our understanding, our power of loving would have been bound up. Had he made it infinite but not prepared objects for it, our love would have been deluded and lost its force. Had he made some objects but not so many as we were capable of loving, love would have been superfluous and dissatisfied. Had he prepared innumerable and endless objects but made them evil, and if he had commanded us to love these evil objects, our love would have been irrational. Had he made more objects than we were able to love, we would have been discontented. But as he made all objects infinitely amiable and glorious, and filled his immensity and eternity with himself and with the luster of his actions, love is an infinite virtue. We see this because nothing is missing but the act of love to enjoy them.

7. If they are all amiable in all respects, they are all according to our hearts' desire in their natures, places, durations, ends, occasions, causes, uses, service, relations, properties, operations, etc. All things, as they immediately proceed from him, are in all respects most perfectly pleasing. And if we have an eye to see and discern this, and a soul able to

receive the benefit, if our nature is so vast and perfect as to see and take pleasure in all their circumstances, then it is the most unreasonable and brutish thing in the world to withdraw our affection from them. It is even worse than diabolical! For we kill ourselves, we blast our happiness, we offend God, we slight the beauty of all his creatures, we break his laws, we act against nature, we darken the light and splendor of our souls, we deface his image, we grieve his love, we do the most vicious and abominable thing that is imaginable. But if we excite and awaken our power, taking in the glory of all objects, then we live open to them, sensible of them, and delight in them. We transform our souls into acts of love and knowledge, we proceed out of ourselves into all immensities and eternities, we render all things their due, and we reap the benefit of all. We are just, wise, and holy. We are grateful to God and amiable in being so; we are not divided from, but united to him, in all his appearances, thoughts, counsels, and operations. We adorn our souls with the beauty of all objects whatsoever and are transformed into the image of God. We live in communion with him, even live in him, and he in us. We are made kings and priests unto God, and his sons forever. There is an exact and pleasant harmony between us and all the creatures: we are in a divine and spiritual manner made, as it were, omnipresent with all objects. The soul is present only by an act of the understanding and becomes the temple of all eternity when the kingdom of God is seated within it as the world is in the eye. While the soul lives, it feels, sees, and enjoys its own and its object's perfection in every object to which it is extended.

8. If by our voluntary carelessness, mistake, or disorder, we dote upon one object, or suffer some few things to engage our souls so entirely, as to forget and neglect all the rest, we rob all those we desert of their due esteem, and abridge ourselves of that liberty and extent in which the greatness of our soul consists. As if the sun, that is made to shine upon all the world, should withdraw its beams from the stars and the heavens, and choose to shine upon nothing else but a spire of grass, a grain of dust, or a little sand. We lose innumerable objects, and confine ourselves to the love of one, by sacrificing all our affection to that, become guilty of idolatry in one respect, of atheism in another. For we elevate that creature which we love alone into the place of God, and we rob the Creator of that supreme affection which is due unto him. And in so doing we bereave ourselves of the sovereign object, in the fruition of which all the rest are happily enjoyed. Thus, when a man so loves his wife or children as to despise all mankind, he forfeits his interest in all kingdoms, and the beauty of all ages is taken from his eyes, his treasures are contracted, and his happiness is maimed and made defective. When a covetous man dotes on his bags of gold, the ambitious on titles of honor, the drunkard on his wine, the lustful goat on his women, the foolish hector on his dice and duels, they banish all other objects, and live as absurdly as if a king should relinquish his crown and confine his thoughts and care to a country manor.[2]

---

[2] Goats are traditionally regarded as lecherous animals, hence the insult being linked with lust here. As for the gambling "hector," this is an archaic word for a bully or braggart. We make little use of this as a noun today, but retain the verb "hectoring."

9. I will not deny that there are many disorders and evils in the world, many deformities, sins, and miseries. But I say two things: first that in the estate of innocence, wherein all things proceeded purely from God, there was no sin, nor sickness, nor death, nor occasion of complaint or calamity. Secondly, that all the evils that are now in the world, men brought on themselves by the fall, and there is great need of distinguishing between the works of God, and the works of men. For all that God did is lovely and divine; nothing is bitter and distasteful, apart from what we have done. He himself surveyed the whole creation and pronounced concerning everything that it was exceedingly good. So that he was in all his works an object of pleasure. To these we add two more considerations. First, that of all the evils and mischiefs which men have introduced, there is not one left uncorrected in his kingdom. Second, that God brings order out of confusion, light out of darkness, good out of evil, and by a providence irresistible, and a power infinite, so limits and divides all, that even evils themselves become part of his victory, the ground of his triumph. They are all improved, and he makes the greatest evils objects of joy and glory.

10. Now, if all things are fit to be enjoyed before God, all good things perfected, all evil overcome; if without any change of place or situation, all things are naked and open before his eyes, and there be no walls to exclude, or screens to hide, no gulf to pass, nor distance to overcome, but all things equally near and far, then there is some hope that the same happiness is prepared for the soul which is made in his image. Everything, being fit for God, is full of infinite depth and beauty. For this reason, St. John being in spirit saw all

the kingdoms of the world become the kingdoms of the Lord and of his Christ, and heard "every created thing which is in heaven, and on the earth, and under the earth, and on the sea, and the things in them, saying, 'To him who sits on the throne and to the Lamb be the blessing, the honor, the glory, and the dominion forever and ever'" [Rev. 5:13]. Then we are rather persuaded to believe this, because the faithful servant is commanded to enter into the joy of his Lord, and our Master's joys are the rewards of believers. Our Savior tells us his Lord will make his wise servant ruler over all his goods in one place, and over all that he has in another [Mt. 25:21].

11. It is the gift of understanding to see beyond all seas, and through all interposing screens and darknesses. To be able to love any object beyond the skies, anything that is good from the center of the earth to the highest heavens, is the property of the soul, which it exercises here by parts and degrees, but shall at once exert at the day of consummation. The infinity of the Father in the Son, and the Godhead of the Son in the Holy Ghost will entirely be enjoyed.

12. It is the glory of man that his avarice is insatiable, and his ambition infinite, that his appetite carries him to innumerable pleasures, and that his curiosity is so endless, that were he monarch of the world, it could not satisfy his soul—still he would be curiously inquisitive into the origins and ends of things, and be concerned in the nature of those that are beyond the heavens. For having met with an infinite benefactor, it would be unfitting if any finite object could satisfy his desire. This is why his reason is so inquisitive, to see whether everything is delightful to his essence—which,

when he finds agreeable to his wish, and to exceed his imagination, it is impossible to declare how his avarice and ambition will both rejoice, how much his appetite will be satisfied, and his curiosity delighted. To sit in the throne of God and to enjoy communion with him in those things which neither eye has seen, nor ear heard, nor has it entered into the heart of man to conceive, is no small thing [1 Cor. 2:9]. The advancement is infinitely greater than we are able to understand. No young man can gaze upon a beautiful face with greater pleasure, no epicure's sense be ravished with more delight, than that which he apprehends in so glorious a fruition.[3]

13. The very sight of other men's souls shining in the acts of their understanding catches the breath in the throat. They shine throughout all eternity, extending themselves in the beams of love through all immensity, and thereby transformed (every one of them) into a sphere of light comprehending the heavens, every angel and every spirit being a temple of God's omnipresence and perfection. This alone will be a ravishing spectacle to that goodness which delights to see innumerable possessors of the same kingdom. Much more will the perfection of the kingdom itself, which by infinite wisdom is so constituted that every one is the sovereign object, the firstborn, and sole heir, and end of the kingdom; every one the bride of God, every one there a king, yet without confusion, or diminution; every one distinctly, enjoying all, and adding to each other's fruition.

---

[3] An "epicure" refers either to someone with refined culinary tastes, or to someone devoted to sensual pleasures.

14. To understand all this, and not to delight in it, is more miserable than not to understand it. To see it without being able to enjoy it is to pine away in a prison, from whence we see the glory of a palace, and repine in our misery at the pleasures of those that are about it. To delight in these things without being affected by them is impossible. There isn't any affection but that of love, whereby we can enjoy them.

15. The angels see the glory of God's kingdom and delight in it. The damned see the joys of the blessed and are tortured by them. The wicked upon earth neither see, nor are affected with them; the saints on earth understand them in part, and believe them, desiring and endeavoring after them. These saints wait with expectation for the whole, and by certain degrees, as it were in a glass, enjoy the image and reflection of them. As much as they comprehend they are able to actually delight in, for their love is awakened and extended to the goodness of all they understand, which it feeds upon by meditation and turns into nourishment for the benefit of their souls, which are made greater, and strong, and vigorous by their fruitions. But without love it is easy to see that no goodness can be at all enjoyed.

16. God does desire love from us, because his wisdom very well knows that without love the world would be in vain, and the end of the creation frustrated. His goodness is diffusive and infinitely desires to communicate itself, which it cannot do unless it is beloved. To receive it is the highest service we can do to it, nothing being more agreeable to the nature of his goodness than that it should be enjoyed. His blessedness consists in the pleasure he takes in the

happiness of others and branches itself out into two parts: the pleasure of communicating all to others, and the pleasure of receiving all from others in the satisfaction which he takes to see others blessed in the returns of those joys and praises, which are offered up to his goodness and glory. His glory desires to be seen and delighted in. To be esteemed and beloved, to be honored and admired, is natural to glory, the brightness of whose splendor is more sensibly pleasant in the reflection of its face, and in the joy that it makes in another's soul. His holiness takes pleasure in pure and upright actions, all which have love as their fountain. There is an objective fitness and excellency in love, for which it is infinitely valued by him. It is one of the first and immediate properties of love to desire to be beloved, to make its object most amiable and beautiful, as well as blessed. Love desires to be united to its object, to have its own goodness acknowledged, its essence approved, its excellence desired, admired, and delighted in; to see all its actions, appearances, gifts, and tokens esteemed, and to feel its own efficacy in the grateful acceptance it finds in the raptures it occasions, in the flames it enkindles in another's soul. Now, love is the fountain of all honor, gratitude, praise, and esteem. By love the soul is transformed into the similitude of God, by love it is made bright and beautiful. All its blessedness and glory are founded in its love; it is by love itself made communicative and diffusive, and great, and rich, and as the Scripture speaks, fit for delights [Song 7:6]. All obedience and service are founded in love; and if a creature that is beloved must freely give itself up to another's pleasure, before it can show its love, or entirely be enjoyed, love is of all other things in the world most fit to answer love, because the very heart and soul is given thereby to the person that desires it.

17. Love is the fountain of all benefits and pleasures. House, estate, lands, authority, wealth, and power—life itself is consecrated and devoted by a lover to his object, so that on our side all is given to God by love, as well as received from him by love. The heavens and the earth and all the creatures are gifts and tokens of his love; men and angels are a present of his love, which he has infinitely adorned, and made endlessly serviceable to every soul that is beloved. His love would have us receive all these with due esteem. Therefore, it is out of his love that he wills us to exercise our reason rightly and love them as much as their goodness deserves. When we see and understand their excellence, and esteem them according to the transcendent value that appears in them, we adorn ourselves with their fair ideas, we enlarge and beautify our souls with bright and clear understanding, and, what is much more, with regular and well-ordered affections, we enrich ourselves, and increase our greatness (in the fruition of his gifts), and become lively, pleasant, vigorous creatures, full of knowledge, and wisdom, and goodness, and fit to offer up all these things unto him again, while we empty them as helps and advantages in that service which we pay unto him. For our love to himself is kindled by these incentives, and while we sacrifice ourselves and them unto him, we delight in nothing more than to see him, who is so great in love and bounty, the Author and Possessor of all his glories.

VIII:
THE EXCELLENCE OF
CHRISTIAN MORALITY

1. I DO NOT see that Aristotle made the end of virtue any other than a finite and temporal happiness, which is infinitely short of that happiness which is begun here and enjoyed forever. He did not make God the object and end of the soul. Further, if all acts are distinguished into their kinds by their objects and their ends, those virtues must be infinitely base that have no other objects or ends but creatures. Only those divine and noble acts that flow from an infinite and eternal origin respect an infinite and eternal object and rest in an infinite and eternal end. Aristotle's definition of happiness imports all this, but his behavior makes me fear he did not understand it. As Seneca luckily hit upon that saying, *deus me solum dedit toto mundo, totum mundum mihi soli*: "God gave me alone to all the world, and all the world to me alone."[1] Yet he could not understand it;

---

[1] Traherne is here giving the sense of a line from Book XX of Seneca's *De Vita Beata*, rather than a direct quote. The relevant lines are rather better rendered: "I shall view all lands as my own, my own as belonging to all others. As for me, I shall always live as if I were aware that I had been born for service to others, and on this account I shall render my thanks to Nature... She has given me, the individual, to all men and all men to me, the

for had he known what it was he said, he would have made a better use of it, and been more verbose and explicit in the illustration. An actual respect for infinite obligations and rewards; a desire in every action to please an infinite and eternal lover, to glorify a divine and endless benefactor, to bring forth the fruits of infinite benefits, and to be truly grateful for all the advantages of a man's creation, that is made to have dominion over all the world; these are higher and better qualifications of those virtuous actions which Christians perform, than heathens understood. And yet if nature were divested of its corruption, the natural man (that is, one who is no Christian) might, by the light of nature, be fitted to understand them. And the truth is, I wonder much (the world being so beautiful and glorious in every eye, so really deep and valuable in worth, so peculiarly applied to the use and service of every person) that the heathens did miss the fruition of it, and fail to measure themselves and their happiness by the greatness of its beauty, and the joy which all the creatures ought to produce in the mind of man by their real services. For the earth is really better than if all its globe were of beaten gold, the seas are better than if all their abysses were full of diamonds, the air is better than if

---

individual... I shall know that the whole world is my country, that its rulers are the gods, and that they abide above me and around me, the censors of my words and deeds." *Moral Essays, Volume II: De Consolatione ad Marciam. De Vita Beata. De Otio. De Tranquillitate Animi. De Brevitate Vitae. De Consolatione ad Polybium. De Consolatione ad Helviam,* trans. John W. Basore, Loeb Classical Library 254 (Cambridge: Harvard University Press, 1932), 151. This idea is also a refrain in Traherne's work *Centuries of Meditation.* For a short summary of Traherne's use of Seneca, see Thomas P. Harrison, "Seneca and Traherne," *Arion: A Journal of Humanities and the Classics* 6, no. 3 (Autumn 1967): 403–5.

all the space between us and the skies were full of scepters, and the sun alone a greater treasure then all the wealthy mines in the Indies. Every man is surrounded with all the light of their advantages, and so much served by them as if no man but himself were alive in the world—to such an extent that it is a natural and easy investigation, even for heathens themselves, to discern the mystery of bliss, and to discover the misery of human nature to be founded in some disease of the will or understanding, and to return from inattentiveness and sloth to truth and right reason, which was the ready way to true happiness. For they knew not the arcane or hidden mystery of divine laws, nor the excellence and perfection of immortal souls, which make everyone a sovereign and transcendent creature. Yet they might easily observe the miserable effects of eternal solitude, and, in external services, how useful and comfortable men were ordained by nature to be to one another.

2. Every man loves to have many eyes fixed on his beauty, and to have many delightful objects and transactions for his own. Be the theater never so magnificent, the actions and the actors are more delightful to the spectators than the gilded walls and dead statues. Were all other men removed out of the world to make room for one, the empty theater would remain, but the spectacle would be lost; all the cities, and kingdoms, and ages would be removed, with all that was lively, and rare, and miraculous in all their occurrences. Palaces and temples would have been prevented, houses and villages, fields and vineyards! The world would have been a wilderness overgrown with thorns, wild beasts, and serpents, which now by the labor of many hands is reduced to the beauty and order of Eden. It is by trades and

occupations that a man gets himself corn, and wine, and oil, etc., all of which he would have been without had he never seen any company but himself, condemned to idleness and melancholy. Virtues and praises would be things unknown; admiration and honor, love and knowledge, the mysteries of religion and piety, all the speculations of wisdom, would be lost for want of education. Or, at least, the *sense and exercise* of these bright and glorious things would have been lost for want of conversation, corrupted nature being prone to afford no other fruits but barbarism and ignorance in that solitary condition. For the powers of the soul are improved by tradition, and it is by the information of others that our minds are awakened to perceive the dignity of our own nature, the value of all the creatures, and our interest in them.

3. But religion teaches us far more. It teaches the beginning and the end of the world, how highly we are honored and beloved of God, the manner wherein we are to converse with him, the transcendent excellency of souls, and the divine perfections of the deity, what his omnipresence and eternity are, how we are to be enlarged in our apprehensions and desires, and prepared for infinite and eternal fruitions. And, what's more, it teaches in what quality and capacity we are to live in the world, and exercise virtue, how we are to spend our time, and employ our powers on all objects, everyone as lord of the creation and the friend of God! Religion teaches how all angels and men are commanded to love us as themselves, and by that love to serve and delight us more than by all other actions and offices whatsoever. It teaches that every soul is a more excellent being than the visible world, more nearly allied to God, and more precious

in itself than any treasure whatsoever. It teaches that it is endued with powers, inclinations, and principles so fitly subservient and conducive to blessedness, that any one of these is more delightful than all inanimate things. In the contemplation and enjoyment of even these inanimate things we may justly be lost in wonder and ecstasy. All this by the light of nature is asserted, but covered with so gross a veil that we discern it not until it is newly revealed by the ministry of men.[2] And upon all these accounts are men themselves, (which are generally mistaken to be impediments) means and assistances of our happy living.

4. But however familiar and near and easy these great and evident truths appear, it so happened that the heathen philosophers were blind to them, and, in the midst of their searches for happiness, failed in their discovery. They became vain in their imaginations, placing happiness in a mere apathy, or conceited self-sufficiency, or in a brave contempt of all misfortunes, in a forced contentment dark and empty, or in sensual pleasures, or in the goods of fortune, either alone, or conjoined with those of the soul and body, which they lamely enumerated, and knew not how to employ—as if the discovery of the highest and best truths in nature had been reserved for him that redeemed nature, and the plainest truths had been appointed to honor

---

[2] The phrase "so gross a veil" is likely a reference to the fourth line of Dante's *Purgatorio* Canto 16: *non fece al viso mio sì grosso velo.* It can perhaps be better rendered "so thick a covering." In this Canto the pilgrims move from smoke-filled darkness and into light. The allusion is intended for the reader. I have chosen to preserve the nod from one poet to another.

and attend that religion which brought supernatural mysteries to light by the preaching of the gospel.

5. By this last element the qualifications of a humble and pious soul, a penitent and grateful person, sensible (at once) of his infinite guilt and grandeur, were introduced; another foundation was laid upon the meritorious death and passion of God, the Son of God; a second love continued in the deity to the miserable after an infinite forfeiture. All the oracles, and visions, and miracles by which the nature of man is magnified and ages enlightened; the ministry of angels and the dispensations of providence, by which the care and tenderness of God is shown; the infinite measures and violences of his love; the infinite variety and number of obligations; the present advantages and benefits; the eternal rewards; the relation of God to man as a father and a friend, a bridegroom and a king, a light and example; the sweetness of our union and communion with him, and the gift of the Holy Ghost sent down from heaven; all these things, which the angels desire to look into, were by the Christian religion (with the rest before mentioned) plainly revealed, with our victory over death, the resurrection of our bodies, and life eternal.

6. In the light of these circumstances the interior form of virtuous acts appears more evidently, and this interiority was hidden from Aristotle and his kind. For to exercise virtue in the quality and capacity of a son of God is another sort of business than to exercise virtue as a mere servant. To do all things being clothed with a sense of our celestial grandeur, as we are heirs of the world, infinitely beloved of God, ordained for his throne, delightful in the eyes of all, angels

and men, beloved and honored by all the creatures, made partakers of the divine nature, intending and designing to please all spectators in heaven and earth (by the excellence of our actions)—this makes every little deed as it were infinite within. While the matter of the action seems nothing, it renders the form divine and blessed.

7. The best actions of the profane heathen were but dead works. By this name the Apostle calls all wicked deeds to intimate the lack of all that excellency which ought to be in human actions [Heb. 6:1]. Every deed and thought of ours ought to be inspired with life from heaven. The light of the understanding, and the vigor of the will, is the soul that informs it. When it is void of knowledge and springs not from that stream of God's infinite love that ought to animate it, or when it lacks regard for those eternal joys that are set before us, or when it fails to consider those obligations that are laid upon us, it is bereaved of its vital and essential form. It is like a fair carcass without a soul, insensible to those interests and concerns that ought chiefly to be valued and promoted. And by this you may see clearly that the matter of a good act falls infinitely short of that perfection with which it ought to be inspired, if this soul or form be wanting, which, though less visible to the eye of flesh, is of as much greater excellence and importance, just as the soul in nature is above the body.

8. Thus, when a heathen gives to the poor, the matter of the act is the very self-same which a Christian man does. So is an act of courage or patience in encountering death, the subduing of the appetite, and the denial of a lust, a piece of justice against interest and friendship, an act of prudence,

temperance, or fidelity. In all these, if we respect the matter of them, heathens have acted (in a manner) as high as any Christian, and consequently appear to vulgar apprehensions as heroic and stupendous. But consider the inside: the heathen did it that he might satisfy his conscience and please the gods, that he might acquire honor and immortal fame, or please the generous inclination of his own soul which delighted in honor and worth, or assert his own principles, or save his friends, or preserve his country. Doubtless these are great and brave considerations, but they are limited and finite, and sick with two defects that (for the most part) are incurable: they were sacrifices of obedience to false gods, plain idolatry, and attended with an ignorant loftiness and height of mind that confided in them. And besides this, they aspired to little more than a glorious name in following ages.

9. In contrast, the Christian makes all kind of graces to meet and concentrate in every action, wisdom, goodness, justice, courage, temperance, prudence, humility, penitence, patience, meekness, liberality, cheerfulness, gratitude, joy in the Holy Ghost, devotion, piety, faith, hope, charity, all kind of holiness, and his action extends to all the objects of these graces and includes their causes. He remembers the infinite obligations that are laid upon him by that deity, who infinitely loves him. He remembers the benefit of the creation, and the glory of the divine image; the guilt of fall, and that blot and misery that lies upon him; the wonder of his redemption and the love of Christ, along with his death and passion; the miraculous pains and endeavors of God in all ages to reclaim him; the giving of the Holy Ghost. And he remembers his holy baptism, the new covenant which he is in with God, the height and glory of his place and station,

the beauty of the world and his dominion over all the living creatures, the joy and goodwill of all the angels, the benefit and welfare of all his neighbors the joy and prosperity of future ages. He remembers the glory of God, the honor of his Church and the propagation of religion, the salvation of others' souls and the eternal state and condition of his own, the acquisition of a celestial and eternal kingdom and the delight he takes in an infinite sphere of eternal joys, the fervent desire he must be grateful to the Almighty. All these by the light of his divine and celestial knowledge enter into every act, for want of which the other work, that is wrought by an ignorant heathen, is in a manner rightly called a work of darkness.

10. I do not state this as if to discourage a heathen from doing the best that he is able, or to condemn those reasons from which he proceeds in his virtuous deeds, or to suggest that grace is necessary to take any action. Rather, I state all this to show how highly Christianity does ennoble the soul of man, how much more sublime its principles are, and how much more perfect it makes his actions when they are what they may be. This ought to provoke Christians to a more intelligent and lofty practice of Christian virtues, lest they differ not in their morals from the better sort of heathens. All these things are necessary to the perfection of an action, though not to its acceptance. God's omnipresence, and power, and wisdom, and love ought to be considered in all places, among all persons, upon all occasions, as well as the blood of Christ and the infinite glory of eternal bliss. But that which above all I chiefly intend is to show what influence the great perfection of happiness has upon all our virtues—not only to stir us up to do them, but, by entering

their constitution, to inspire them with their beauty and form for their fuller luster, glory, and perfection, that we may also see how great and transcendent that life must be in which every act is capable of so much majesty and magnificence, if I may so speak, by reason of the variety of its ends and causes. And I intend also to show how abominable and absurd are all those that exclude God out of their thoughts and considerations, who is alone the fountain of all the beauty in every virtuous deed, and the proper fullness, cause and end of all its perfection!

11. How ambitious we ought to be for knowledge, which is the light in which we are to adorn and complete ourselves. We may learn and collect from all that is said. It is rightly called "the key of knowledge." It admits us into the spacious recesses of every virtue, and opens the gate by which we enter into the paths of righteousness that lead to the temple and palace of bliss where all the treasuries of wisdom are exposed to the eye of the soul, though hidden from the world. How great and amiable every virtue is, how great and perfect it may be made, is only discerned by the eye of knowledge. It is by this alone that men come to discern how full of reason religion is, and with what joy and security and sweetness it may be practiced.

MORE FROM DAVENANT PRESS

INTRODUCTION TO PROTESTANT THEOLOGY
Reformation Theology: A Reader of Primary Sources with Introductions
Grace Worth Fighting For: Recapturing the Vision of God's Grace in the Canons of Dordt

PETER MARTYR VERMIGLI LIBRARY
Dialogue on the Two Natures in Christ
Philosophical Works: On the Relation of Philosophy to Theology
The Oxford Treatise and Disputation on the Eucharist, 1549
Predestination and Justification: Two Theological Loci

VERMIGLI'S *COMMON PLACES*
On Original Sin (Vol. 1)
On Free Will and the Law (Vol. 2)

LIBRARY OF EARLY ENGLISH PROTESTANTISM
James Ussher and a Reformed Episcopal Church: Sermons and Treatises on Ecclesiology
The Apology of the Church of England
Jurisdiction Regal, Episcopal, Papal
Radicalism: When Reform Becomes Revolution
Divine Law and Human Nature
The Word of God and the Words of Man
In Defense of Reformed Catholic Worship
A Learned Discourse on Justification
The Laws of Ecclesiastical Polity: In Modern English, Vol. 1 (Preface–Book IV)

DAVENANT GUIDES
Jesus and Pacifism: An Exegetical and Historical Investigation

The Two Kingdoms: A Guide for the Perplexed
Natural Law: A Brief Introduction and Biblical Defense
Natural Theology: A Biblical and Historical Introduction and Defense

DAVENANT RETRIEVALS
A Protestant Christendom? The World the Reformation Made
People of the Promise: A Mere Protestant Ecclesiology
Philosophy and the Christian: The Quest for Wisdom in the Light of Christ
The Lord Is One: Reclaiming Divine Simplicity

CONVIVIUM PROCEEDINGS
For the Healing of the Nations: Essays on Creation, Redemption, and Neo-Calvinism
For Law and for Liberty: Essays on the Legacy of Protestant Political Thought
Beyond Calvin: Essays on the Diversity of the Reformed Tradition
God of Our Fathers: Classical Theism for the Contemporary Church
Reforming the Catholic Tradition: The Whole Word for the Whole Church
Reforming Classical Education: Toward A New Paradigm

OTHER PUBLICATIONS
Enduring Divine Absence: The Challenge of Modern Atheism
Without Excuse: Scripture, Reason, and Presuppositional Apologetics
Being A Pastor: Pastoral Treatises of John Wycliffe
Serious Comedy: The Philosophical and Theological Significance of Tragic and Comic Writing in the Western Tradition
Protestant Social Teaching: An Introduction
Begotten or Made?

ABOUT THE LIBRARY OF EARLY ENGLISH PROTESTANTISM

The Library of Early English Protestantism (LEEP) is a multi-year project that aims to make available in scholarly but accessible editions seminal writings from key but neglected sixteenth- and seventeenth-century Church of England theologians. This project intends to bring old resources to a new audience, specifically for those Reformed and Anglican readers seeking to deepen and broaden their understanding of their theological tradition. The purpose of LEEP is to make the rediscovery of these sources as easy as possible by providing affordable, comprehensively-edited, modernized-spelling editions for contemporary seminarians, clergy, students, and theologically-concerned laypeople.

ABOUT THE DAVENANT INSTITUTE

The Davenant Institute supports the renewal of Christian wisdom for the contemporary church. It seeks to sponsor historical scholarship at the intersection of the church and academy, build networks of friendship and collaboration within the Reformed and evangelical world, and equip the saints with time-tested resources for faithful public witness.

We are a nonprofit organization supported by your tax-deductible gifts. Learn more about us, and donate, at www.davenantinstitute.org.